Insights You Need from
Harvard Business Review

WEB3

Insights You Need from Harvard Business Review

Business is changing. Will you adapt or be left behind?

Get up to speed and deepen your understanding of the topics that are shaping your company's future with the **Insights You Need from Harvard Business Review** series. Featuring HBR's smartest thinking on fast-moving issues—blockchain, cybersecurity, AI, and more—each book provides the foundation introduction and practical case studies your organization needs to compete today and collects the best research, interviews, and analysis to get it ready for tomorrow.

You can't afford to ignore how these issues will transform the landscape of business and society. The Insights You Need series will help you grasp these critical ideas—and prepare you and your company for the future.

Books in the series include:

Agile	*Global Recession*
Artificial Intelligence	*Hybrid Workplace*
Blockchain	*Monopolies and Tech Giants*
Climate Change	
Coronavirus: Leadership and Recovery	*Racial Justice*
Customer Data and Privacy	*Strategic Analytics*
	The Year in Tech, 2021
Cybersecurity	*The Year in Tech, 2022*
Crypto	*The Year in Tech, 2023*
The Future of Work	*Web3*

Insights You Need from
Harvard Business Review

WEB3

Harvard Business Review Press
Boston, Massachusetts

Copyright 2023 Harvard Business School Publishing Corporation
All rights reserved
Printed in the United States of America

10 9 8 7 6 5 4 3 2 1

No part of this publication may be reproduced, stored in or introduced into a retrieval system, or transmitted, in any form, or by any means (electronic, mechanical, photocopying, recording, or otherwise), without the prior permission of the publisher. Requests for permission should be directed to permissions@hbsp .harvard.edu, or mailed to Permissions, Harvard Business School Publishing, 60 Harvard Way, Boston, Massachusetts 02163.

The web addresses referenced in this book were live and correct at the time of the book's publication but may be subject to change.

Library of Congress Cataloging-in-Publication Data

Names: Harvard Business Review Press, issuing body.
Title: Web3.
Other titles: Insights you need from Harvard Business Review.
Description: Boston, Massachusetts : Harvard Business Review Press, [2023] | Series: Insights you need from Harvard Business Review | Includes bibliographical references and index.
Identifiers: LCCN 2022039362 (print) | LCCN 2022039363 (ebook) | ISBN 9781647824976 (paperback) | ISBN 9781647824983 (epub)
Subjects: LCSH: World Wide Web—Technological innovations. | Business—Data processing. | Blockchains (Databases)—Industrial applications. | Cryptocurrencies. | Web applications.
Classification: LCC TK5105.888 .W36746 2023 (print) | LCC TK5105.888 (ebook) | DDC 004.67/8—dc23/eng/20221103
LC record available at https://lccn.loc.gov/2022039362
LC ebook record available at https://lccn.loc.gov/2022039363

ISBN: 978-1-64782-497-6
eISBN: 978-1-64782-498-3

The paper used in this publication meets the requirements of the American National Standard for Permanence of Paper for Publications and Documents in Libraries and Archives Z39.48-1992.

Contents

Contents

Introduction

WHAT IS WEB3?

by Thomas Stackpole

Do you remember the first time you heard about Bitcoin? Maybe it was a faint buzz about a new technology that would change everything. Perhaps you felt a tingle of FOMO as the folks who got in early suddenly amassed a small fortune—even if it wasn't clear what the "money" could legitimately be spent on. Maybe you just wondered whether your company should be working on a crypto strategy in case it *did* take off in your industry, even if you didn't really care one way or the other about it.

Most likely, soon after Bitcoin came to your attention— whenever that may have happened—there was a crash. Every year or two, Bitcoin's value has tanked. Each time it does, skeptics rush to dismiss it as dead, railing that it was always a scam for nerds and crooks and was nothing more than a fringe curiosity pushed by techno-libertarians and people who hate banks. Bitcoin never had a future alongside *real* tech companies, they'd contend, and then they'd forget about it and move on with their lives.

And, of course, it would come back.

Bitcoin now seems to be everywhere. Amid all the demands on our attention, many of us didn't notice cryptocurrencies slowly seeping into the mainstream. Until suddenly Larry David was pitching them during the Super Bowl; stars like Paris Hilton, Tom Brady, and Jamie Foxx were hawking them in ads; and a frankly terrifying Wall Street–inspired robot bull celebrating cryptocurrency was unveiled in Miami. What was first a curiosity and then a speculative niche has become big business—although that hasn't stopped it from crashing yet again.

Crypto, however, is just the tip of the spear. The underlying technology, blockchain, is what's called a "distributed ledger"—a database hosted by a network of computers instead of a single server—that offers users an immutable and transparent way to store information. Blockchain is now being deployed to new ends: for instance, to create "digital deed" ownership records of unique digital objects—or non-fungible tokens. NFTs exploded in 2021 and 2022, conjuring a $41 billion market seemingly out of thin air. Beeple, for example, caused a sensation when an NFT of his artwork sold for $69 million at Christie's. Even more esoteric cousins, such as DAOs, or "decentralized autonomous organizations," operate like headless corporations: They raise and spend money, but all decisions are voted on by members and executed by encoded rules. One DAO recently raised $47 million in an attempt to buy a rare copy of the U.S. Constitution. Advocates of DeFi (or "decentralized finance," which aims to remake the global financial system) are lobbying Congress and pitching a future without banks.

The totality of these efforts is called "Web3." The moniker is a convenient shorthand for the project of rewiring how the web works, using blockchain to change how information is stored, shared, and owned. In theory, a blockchain-based web could shatter the monopolies on who controls information, who makes money, and even how networks and corporations work. Advocates argue that Web3 will create new economies, new classes of products, and new services online; that it will return democracy to the web; that it is going to define the next era of the internet—that it is inevitable.

Or is it? While it's undeniable that energy, money, and talent are surging into Web3 projects, remaking the web is a major undertaking. For all its promise, blockchain faces significant technical, environmental, ethical, and regulatory hurdles between here and hegemony. A growing chorus of skeptics warns that Web3 is rotten with speculation, theft, and privacy problems, and that the pull of centralization and the proliferation of new intermediaries is already undermining the utopian pitch for a decentralized web.

Meanwhile, businesses and leaders are trying to make sense of the potential—and pitfalls—of a rapidly changing landscape that could pay serious dividends to organizations that get it right. Many companies are testing the Web3 waters, and while some have enjoyed major successes, several high-profile firms are finding that they (or their customers) don't like the temperature. Most people, of course, don't even really know what Web3 is: In a casual poll of *Harvard Business Review* readers on LinkedIn in 2022, almost 70% said they didn't know what the term meant.

Welcome to the confusing, contested, exciting, utopian, scam-ridden, disastrous, democratizing, (maybe) decentralized world of Web3. Here's what you need to know.

From Web1 to Web3

To put Web3 into context, let me offer a quick refresher.

In the beginning, there was the internet: the physical infrastructure of wires and servers that lets computers, and the people in front of them, talk to each other. The U.S. government's Arpanet sent its first message in 1969, but the web as we know it today didn't emerge until 1991, when HTML and URLs made it possible for users to navigate between static pages. Consider this the read-only web, or Web1.

In the early 2000s, things started to change. For one, the internet was becoming more interactive; it was an era of user-generated content, or the read/write web. Social media was a key feature of Web2 (or Web 2.0, as you may know it), and Facebook, Twitter, and Tumblr came to define the experience of being online. YouTube, Wikipedia, and Google, along with the ability to comment on content, expanded our ability to watch, learn, search, and communicate.

The Web2 era has also been one of centralization. Network effects and economies of scale have led to clear winners, and those companies (many of which I mentioned above) have produced mind-boggling wealth for themselves and their shareholders by scraping users' data and selling targeted ads against it. This has allowed services to be offered for "free," though users initially didn't understand the implications of that bargain. Web2 also created new ways for regular people to make money, such as through the sharing economy and the sometimes-lucrative job of being an influencer.

There's plenty to critique in the current system: The companies with concentrated or near-monopoly power have often failed to wield it responsibly, consumers who now realize that they *are* the product are becoming increasingly uncomfortable with ceding control of their personal data, and it's possible that the targeted-ad economy is a fragile bubble that does little to actually boost advertisers. As the web has grown up, centralized, and gone corporate, many have started to wonder whether there's a better future out there.

Which brings us to Web3. Advocates of this vision are pitching it as a roots-deep update that will correct the problems and perverse incentives of Web2. Worried about privacy? Encrypted wallets protect your online identity. About censorship? A decentralized database stores everything immutably and transparently, preventing moderators from swooping in to delete offending content. Centralization? You get a real vote on decisions made by the networks you spend time on. More than that, you get a stake that's *worth something*—you're not a product, you're an owner. This is the vision of the read/write/own web.

OK, but What *Is* Web3?

The seeds of what would become Web3 were planted in 1991, when scientists W. Scott Stornetta and Stuart Haber launched the first blockchain—a project to timestamp digital documents. But the idea didn't really take root until 2009, when Bitcoin was launched in the wake of the financial crisis (and at least partially in response to it) by the pseudonymous inventor Satoshi Nakamoto. It and its undergirding blockchain technology work like this: Ownership of the cryptocurrency is tracked on a shared public ledger, and when one user wants to make a transfer, "miners" process the transaction by solving a complex math problem, adding a new "block" of data to the chain, and earning newly created Bitcoin for their efforts. While the Bitcoin chain is used just for currency, newer blockchains offer other options. Ethereum, which launched in 2015, is both a cryptocurrency and a platform that can be used to build other cryptocurrencies and blockchain projects. Gavin Wood, one of its cofounders, described Ethereum as "one computer for the entire planet," with computing power distributed across the globe and controlled nowhere. Now, after more than a decade, proponents of a blockchain-based web are proclaiming that a new era—Web3—has dawned.

Put *very* simply, Web3 is an extension of cryptocurrency, using blockchain in new ways to new ends. A blockchain can store the number of tokens in a wallet, the terms of a self-executing contract, or the code for a decentralized app (dApp). Not all blockchains work the same way, but in general, coins are used as incentives for miners to process transactions. On proof-of-work chains

Glossary of Web3 Terms

Web3. A new version of the web, built on blockchains, that would (in theory) be decentralized, democratic, and peer-to-peer. Cryptocurrencies, NFTs, and DAOs are all part of the Web3 and enable a read/write/own internet.

Blockchain. A "distributed ledger"—that is, a database hosted by a network of computers instead of a single server—that offers users an immutable and transparent way to store information. It's the backbone for Web3 technologies like cryptocurrencies and NFTs.

Cryptocurrency. A form of currency that doesn't rely on a central bank, government, or other intermediaries. Technically, it's a software that runs on blockchains. There are currently thousands of cryptocurrencies, but the most common include bitcoin and ether.

like Bitcoin, solving the complex math problems necessary to process transactions is energy-intensive by design. On a "proof of stake" chain, which is newer but increasingly common, processing transactions simply requires that the verifiers with a stake in the chain agree that a transaction is legit—a process that's significantly more efficient. In

NFT (non-fungible token). An NFT is a digital deed representing ownership over a unique digital object. These objects commonly include artwork or digital versions of collectibles such as the illustrated avatars of the Bored Ape Yacht Club or *Time* magazine covers. They are authenticated on a blockchain.

DAO (decentralized autonomous organization). A DAO is a headless corporation that raises and spends money. All decisions are voted on by members and executed by encoded rules on a blockchain. They are often formed by congregations of strangers who are geographically dispersed but share a common goal.

both cases, transaction data is public, though users' wallets are identified only by a cryptographically generated address. Blockchains are "write only," which means you can add data to them but can't delete it.

Web3 and cryptocurrencies run on what are called "permissionless" blockchains, which have no centralized control and don't require users to trust—or even know anything about—other users to do business with them. This is mostly what people are talking about when they say "blockchain." "Web3 is the internet owned by the builders and users, orchestrated with tokens," says Chris Dixon, a partner at the venture capital firm a16z and one of Web3's foremost advocates and investors, borrowing the definition from Web3 adviser Packy McCormick. This is a big deal because it changes a foundational dynamic of today's web, in which companies squeeze users for every bit of data they can. Tokens and shared ownership, Dixon says, fix "the core problem of centralized networks, where the value is accumulated by one company, and the company ends up fighting its own users and partners."

In 2014, Ethereum's Wood wrote a foundational blog post in which he sketched out his view of the new era. Web3 is a "reimagination of the sorts of things we already use the web for, but with a fundamentally different model for the interactions between parties," he said. "Information that we assume to be public, we publish. Information that we assume to be agreed, we place on a consensus-ledger. Information that we assume to be private, we keep secret and never reveal." In this vision, all communication is encrypted, and identities are hidden. "In short, we engineer the system to mathematically enforce our prior assumptions, since no government or organization can reasonably be trusted."

The idea has evolved since then, and new use cases have started popping up. The Web3 streaming service Sound. xyz promises a better deal for artists. Blockchain-based games, like the Pokémon-esque *Axie Infinity*, let users earn money as they play. So-called stablecoins, whose value is pegged to the dollar, the euro, or some other external reference, have been pitched as upgrades to the global financial system (though not all of them remained stable, or even solvent, through the May 2022 crash). And crypto has gained traction as a solution for cross-border payments, especially for users in volatile environments.

"Blockchain is a new type of computer," Dixon tells me. Just as it took years to understand the extent to which PCs and smartphones transformed the way we use technology, blockchain has been in a long incubation phase. Now, he says, "I think we might be in the golden period of Web3, where all the entrepreneurs are entering." Although the eye-popping price tags, like the Beeple sale, have garnered much of the attention, there's more to the story. "The vast majority of what I'm seeing is smaller-dollar things that are much more around communities," he notes, like Sound.xyz. Whereas scale has been a key measure of a Web2 company, engagement is a better indicator of what might succeed in Web3.

Dixon is betting big on this future. He and a16z (a venture capital firm) started putting money into the space in 2013 and invested $2.2 billion in Web3 companies in 2021 and said he was looking to double that the following year.[1] The number of active developers working on Web3 code nearly doubled in 2021, to roughly 18,000—not huge, considering global numbers, but notable, nonetheless. Perhaps most significantly, Web3 projects have become part of the zeitgeist, and the buzz is undeniable.

But as high-profile, self-immolating startups like Theranos and WeWork remind us, buzz isn't everything. So what happens next? And what should you watch out for?

What Web3 Might Mean for Companies

Web3 will have a few key differences from Web2: Users won't need separate log-ins for every site they visit but instead will use a centralized identity (probably their crypto wallet) that carries their information. They'll have more control over the sites they visit, as they earn or buy tokens that allow them to vote on decisions or unlock functionality.

It's still unclear whether the product lives up to the pitch. Predictions as to what Web3 might look like at scale are just guesses, but some projects have grown pretty big.

The Bored Ape Yacht Club, NBA Top Shot, and the cryptogaming giant Dapper Labs have built successful NFT communities. Clearinghouses such as Coinbase (for buying, selling, and storing cryptocurrency) and OpenSea (the largest digital marketplace for crypto collectibles and NFTs) have created Web3 on-ramps for people with little to no technical know-how.

While companies such as Microsoft, Overstock, and PayPal have accepted cryptocurrencies for years, NFTs are the primary way brands are now experimenting with Web3. Practically speaking, an NFT is some mix of a deed, a certificate of authenticity, and a membership card. It can confer "ownership" of digital art (typically, ownership is recorded on the blockchain and a link points to an image somewhere) or rights or access to a group. NFTs can operate on a smaller scale than coins because they create their own ecosystems and require nothing more than a community of people who find value in the project. For example, baseball cards are valuable only to certain collectors, but that group *really* believes in their value.

Most successful forays by traditional companies into Web3 have been ones that create communities or plug in to existing ones. Consider the NBA: Top Shot was one of the first NFT projects from a legacy brand, and it offered fans the opportunity to buy and trade clips, called "moments" (a LeBron James dunk, for instance), that function like trading cards. It took off because it created a new kind of community space for fans, many of whom may have already been collecting basketball cards. Other front-runner brands, such as Nike, Adidas, and Under Armour, similarly added a digital layer to their existing collector communities. All three companies offer NFTs that can be used in the virtual world—for example, allowing the owner to gear up an avatar—or that confer rights to products or exclusive streetwear drops in the real world. Adidas sold $23 million worth of NFTs in less than a day and instantly created a resale market on OpenSea, just like what you might see after a limited drop of new shoes. Similarly, *Time* magazine launched an NFT project to build an online community that leverages the publication's deep history.

Bored Ape Yacht Club is the biggest success story of an NFT project going mainstream. Combining hype and exclusivity, BAYC offers access to real-life parties and to online spaces, along with usage rights to the ape's image—further reinforcing the brand. An ape NFT puts the owner in an exclusive club, both figuratively and literally.

One lesson from these efforts is that on-ramps matter, but less so the more committed the community is. Getting a crypto wallet isn't hard, but it is an added step. So Top Shot doesn't require a one—users can just plug in their credit card—which helped it acquire interested users new to NFTs. The BAYC was a niche interest, but when it took off, it became a catalyst for people to create wallets and drove interest in OpenSea.

Some companies have had rockier experiences with NFT projects and crypto features. For example, when Jason Citron, the CEO of Discord, a voice, video, and text communication service, teased a feature that could connect the app to crypto wallets, Discord users mutinied, leading him to clarify that the company had "no current plans" to launch the tie-in. The underwear brand MeUndies and the U.K. branch of the World Wildlife Fund both quickly pulled the plug on NFT projects after a fierce backlash by customers furious about their sizable carbon footprint. Even the success stories have hit bumps in the road. Nike is currently fighting to have unauthorized NFTs "destroyed," and OpenSea is full of knockoffs and imitators. Given that blockchain is immutable, this is raising novel legal questions, and it isn't clear how companies will handle the issue. Further, there's recent evidence that the market for NFTs is stalling entirely.

Companies that are considering stepping into this space should remember: Web3 is polarizing, and there are no guarantees. Amid many points of disagreement, the chief divide is between people who believe in what Web3 *could* be and critics who decry the many problems dogging it right now.

The Case Against Web3

The early days of a technology are a heady time. The possibilities are endless, and there's a focus on what it can do—or *will* do, according to optimists. I'm old enough to remember when the unfettered discourse enabled by Twitter and Facebook was supposed to sow democracy the world over. As Web3's aura of inevitability (and profitability) wins converts, it's important to consider what could go wrong and recognize what's *already* going wrong.

It's rife with speculation

Skeptics argue that for all the rhetoric about democratization, ownership opportunities, and mass wealth building, Web3 is nothing more than a giant speculative economy that will mostly make some already-rich people even richer. It's easy to see why this argument makes sense. The top 0.01% of bitcoin holders own 27% of the supply. Wash trading, or selling assets to yourself, and market manipulation have been reported in both crypto and NFT markets, artificially pumping up value and allowing owners to earn coins through sham trades. In an interview on the podcast *The Dig*, reporters

Edward Ongweso Jr. and Jacob Silverman characterized the whole system as an elaborate upward transfer of wealth.[2] Writing in the *Atlantic*, investor Rex Woodbury called Web3 "the financialization of everything" (and not in a good way).[3] On a more granular level, Molly White, a software engineer, created Web3 Is Going Just Great, where she tracks the many hacks, scams, and implosions in the Web3 world, underscoring the pitfalls of the unregulated, Wild West territory (read an interview with White in chapter 6 of this book).

The unpredictable, speculative nature of the markets may be a feature, not a bug. According to technologist David Rosenthal, speculation on cryptocurrencies is the engine that drives Web3—that it can't work without it. "[A] permissionless blockchain *requires* a cryptocurrency to function, and this cryptocurrency *requires* speculation to function," he said in a talk at Stanford in early 2022.[4] Basically, he's describing a pyramid scheme: Blockchains need to give people something in exchange for volunteering computing power, and cryptocurrencies fill that role—but the system works only if other people are willing to buy them believing that they'll be worth more in the future. Stephen Diehl, a technologist and vocal critic of Web3, floridly dismissed blockchain as "a one-trick pony whose only application is creating censorship-resistant crypto investment schemes, an invention whose negative externalities and capacity for harm vastly outweigh any possible uses."[5]

The tech isn't practical (and it's *expensive*)

Questions abound as to whether Web3—or blockchain, really—makes sense as the technology that will define the web's next era. "Whether or not you agree with the philosophy/economics behind cryptocurrencies, they are—simply put—a software architecture disaster in the making," says Grady Booch, chief scientist for software engineering at IBM Research. All technology comes with trade-offs, Booch explained in a Twitter Spaces conversation, and the cost of a "trustless" system is that it's highly inefficient, capable of processing only a few transactions per minute—tiny amounts of data compared with a centralized system like, say, Amazon Web Services. Decentralization makes technology more complicated and further out of reach for basic users, rather than simpler and more accessible.

While it's possible to fix this by adding new layers that can speed things up, doing so makes the whole system more centralized, which defeats the purpose. Moxie Marlinspike, founder of the encrypted messaging app Signal, put it this way: "Once a distributed ecosystem centralizes around a platform for convenience, it becomes the worst of both worlds: centralized control, but still distributed enough to become mired in time."[6]

For now, the inefficiency of blockchain comes at a cost, quite literally. Transaction costs on Bitcoin and Ethereum (which calls them gas fees) can run anywhere from a few bucks to hundreds of dollars. Storing one megabyte of data on a blockchain distributed ledger can cost thousands, or even tens of thousands, of dollars—yes, you read that correctly. That's why the NFT you bought probably isn't actually on a blockchain. The code on the chain indicating your ownership includes an address, pointing to where the image is stored. Which can and has caused problems, including your pricy purchase disappearing if the server it *actually* lives on goes down.

It enables harassment and abuse

The potential for disastrous unintended consequences is very real. "While blockchain proponents speak about a 'future of the web' based around public ledgers, anonymity, and immutability," writes Molly White, "those of us who have been harassed online look on in horror as obvious vectors for harassment and abuse are overlooked, if not outright touted as features."[7] Although crypto wallets theoretically provide anonymity, the fact that transactions are public means that they can be traced back to individuals. (The FBI is pretty good at doing this, which is why crypto isn't great for criminal enterprise.) "Imagine if, when you Venmo-ed your Tinder date for your half of the meal, they could now see every other transaction you'd ever made," including with other dates, your therapist, and the corner store by your house. That information in the hands of an abusive ex-partner or a stalker could be life-threatening.

The immutability of the blockchain also means that data can't be taken down. There's no way to erase anything, whether it's a regrettable post or revenge porn. Immutability also could spell major problems for Web3 in some places, such as Europe, where the General Data Protection Regulation (GDPR) enshrines the right to have personal data erased.

It's currently terrible for the environment

Web3's environmental impact is vast and deeply damaging. It can be broken into two categories: energy use and tech waste, both of which are products of mining. Running a network that depends on supercomputers competing to solve complex equations every time you want to save data on a blockchain takes a tremendous amount of energy. It also generates e-waste: According to Rosenthal, Bitcoin produces "an average of one whole MacBook Air of e-waste per 'economically meaningful' transaction" as miners cycle through quantities of short-lived computer hardware. The research he bases this claim on, by Alex de Vries and Christian Stoll, found that the annual e-waste created by Bitcoin is comparable to the amount produced by a country the size of the Netherlands.[8]

Whether and how these issues will be addressed is hard to say, in part because it's still unclear whether Web3 will really catch on. Blockchain is a technology in search of a real use, says technology writer Evgeny Morozov. "The business model of most Web3 ventures is self-referential in the extreme, feeding off people's faith in the inevitable transition from Web2 to Web3." Tim O'Reilly, who coined "Web 2.0" to describe the platform web of the early 2000s, claims that we're in an investment boom reminiscent of the dot-com era before the bottom fell out. "Web 2.0 was not a version number, it was the second coming of the web after the dot-com bust," he says. "I don't think we're going to be able to call Web3 'Web3' until after the crypto bust. Because only then will we get to see what's stuck around."[9]

If that's true, then innovation is going to come at significant cost. As Hilary Allen, an American University law professor who studies the 2008 financial crisis, points out, the system now "mirrors and magnifies the fragilities of shadow banking innovations that resulted in the 2008 financial crisis." If the Web3 bubble bursts, it could leave a lot of folks high and dry.

Early Days Are Here Again

So, where exactly is Web3 headed? Ethereum cofounder Vitalik Buterin has expressed concerns about the direction his creation has taken but continues to be optimistic. In a response to Marlinspike on the Ethereum Reddit page, he conceded that the Signal founder presented "a correct criticism of the *current state* of the ecosystem" but maintained that the decentralized web is catching up, and pretty quickly at that.[10] The work being done now—creating libraries of code—will soon make it easier for other developers to start working on Web3 projects. "I think the properly authenticated decentralized blockchain world is coming and is much closer to being here than many people think."

For one, proof of work—the inefficient-by-design system Bitcoin runs on—is falling out of vogue. Instead of mining, which uses intensive amounts of energy, validation increasingly comes from users buying in (owning a stake) to approve transactions. Ethereum's September 2022 transition to proof of stake cut it's energy usage by an estimated 99.95%, while making the platform faster and more efficient. Solana, a newer blockchain that uses proof of stake and "proof of history," a mechanism that relies on time stamps, can process 65,000 transactions per second (compared with Bitcoin's current rate of about 7 per second.) and uses about as much energy as two Google searches—consumption it buys carbon offsets for.

Some companies are adopting a hybrid approach to blockchain, which offers the benefits without the constraints. "There are a lot of really interesting new architectures, which put certain things on the blockchain but not others," he tells me. A social network, for instance, could record your followers and who you follow on the blockchain, but not your posts, giving you the option to delete them.

Hybrid models can also help companies address GDPR and other regulations. "To comply with the right to erasure," explain Cindy Compert, Maurizio Luinetti, and Bertrand Portier in an IBM white paper, "personal data should be kept private from the blockchain in an 'off-chain' data store, with only its evidence (cryptographic hash) exposed to the chain."[11] That way, personal data can be deleted in keeping with GDPR without affecting the chain.

For better or worse, regulation is coming—slowly—and it will define the next chapter of Web3. China has banned cryptocurrencies outright, along with Algeria, Bangladesh, Egypt, Iraq, Morocco, Oman, Qatar, and Tunisia. Europe is considering environmental regulations that would curb or ban proof-of-work blockchains. In the United States, the Biden administration issued an executive order in early 2022 directing the federal government to look into regulating cryptocurrencies.

With so much of Web3 still being hashed out, it remains a high-risk, high-reward bet. Certain companies and sectors have more incentive than others to try their luck, particularly those that got burned by being left out in earlier eras of the web. It's not a coincidence that a media company like Time Media Group is interested in the opportunities of Web3 after Web2 decimated its business model. Other organizations—like Nike and the NBA, which already have experience with limited drops and commoditizing moments—may have simply found that their business models are an easy fit. Other businesses won't have as clear a path.

The soaring claims around Web3—that it will take over the internet, upend the financial system, redistribute wealth, and make the web democratic again—should be taken with a grain of salt. We've heard all this before, and we've seen how earlier episodes of Web3 euphoria fizzled. But that doesn't mean it should be written off entirely. Maybe it booms, maybe it busts, but we'll be living with some form of it either way. What version—and how your company responds—could determine the future of the digital economy and what life online looks like for the next internet epoch. For now, that future is still up for grabs. Nothing, after all, is inevitable.

TAKEAWAYS

Web3 is being touted as a new version of the web that will be decentralized, democratic, and peer-to-peer. Potential, opportunities, and grand visions for the future abound, but companies should consider both the risks and the rewards before diving in.

✓ The Web2 era, which began in the early 2000s, was a time of centralization on the web. Giant tech companies grew to wield near-monopoly power with "free" services.

✓ Blockchain-based Web3 has been called a "read/write/own" internet that can provide better identity protection, avoid censorship, and grant users voting and ownership stakes in the communities they participate in.

✓ Hallmarks of Web3 are likely to include the use of cryptocurrencies, NFTs (non-fungible tokens), DAOs (decentralized autonomous organizations), and DeFi (decentralized finance).

✓ Skeptics have pointed out that the blockchain-based web has substantial technical, environmental, ethical, privacy, accessibility, and regulatory hurdles—including inaccessibility to basic users, financial exclusion, enabling of harassment and abuse, and negative environmental impact.

NOTES

1. Hannah Murphy, "Andreessen Horowitz Bet on Crypto 'Golden Era' with New $4.5bn Fund," *Financial Times*, May 25, 2022, https://www.ft.com/content/47b05080-67ac-4468-b530-76325d6aba35.

2. Edward Ongweso Jr. and Jacob Silverman, "Cryptocurrency," December 16, 2021, *The Dig*, podcast, https://thedigradio.com/podcast/cryptocurrency-w-edward-ongweso-jr-jacob-silverman/.

3. Rex Woodbury, "What Happens When You're the Investment," *Atlantic*, November 9, 2021.

4. David Rosenthal, "EE380 Talk," *DSHR's Blog* (blog), February 9, 2022, https://blog.dshr.org/2022/02/ee380-talk.html.

5. Stephen Diehl, "Web3 is Bullshit," *Stephen Diehl* (blog), December 4, 2021, https://www.stephendiehl.com/blog/web3 -bullshit.html.

6. "My first impressions of web3," *Moxie Marlinspike* (blog), January 7, 2022, https://moxie.org/2022/01/07/web3-first -impressions.html.

7. Molly White, "Abuse and harassment on the blockchain," *Molly White* (blog), January 22, 2022, https://blog.mollywhite.net/abuse -and-harassment-on-the-blockchain/.

8. Alex de Vries and Christian Stoll, "Bitcoin's growing e-waste problem," *Resources, Conservation and Recycling* 175 (2021).

9. Mark Sullivan, "Web pioneer Tim O'Reilly on Web3," *Fast Company, February* 3, 2022, https://www.fastcompany.com /90716841/tim-oreilly-on-web3.

10. Andrew R. Chow, "Ethereum's Vitalik Buterin Is Worried About Crypto's Future," *Time*, March 18, 2022, https://time.com /6158182/vitalik-buterin-ethereum-profile/.

11. Cindy Compert, Maurizio Luinetti, and Bertrand Portier, "Blockchain and GDPR," IBM white paper, March 2018, iapp.org.

Adapted from content posted on hbr.org, May 10, 2022 (product #H070UE).

1

WEB3 WILL RUN ON CRYPTOCURRENCY

An interview with Jeff John Roberts by Ramsey Khabbaz

What could Web3, an internet ecosystem based on blockchains, crypto wallets, NFTs, and DAOs mean for business? As we hurtle forward, it's important to pause and consider how we got here. To help HBR's readers understand the origins of cryptocurrencies, think through their present problems, and situate them in a Web3 context, I spoke with Jeff John Roberts, a technology journalist and the author of *Kings of Crypto: One Startup's Quest to Take Cryptocurrency out of Silicon Valley and onto Wall Street*. Roberts is also crypto editor at *Fortune*. This interview has been edited.

HBR: *Many people hear "crypto" and immediately think Bitcoin—maybe Dogecoin or Ethereum—but obviously the term encompasses much more than that. Help me understand the basics of what crypto is, broadly, and why it's so important today.*

JOHN JEFF ROBERTS: Crypto is kind of an amorphous term. In essence, it's software that runs blockchains. And blockchains are just ledgers that record every transaction that occurs. This means that they're tamper-proof, distributed, and immutable. That might sound like a lot of jargon, but it's really just the notion of running the same computer program on multiple computers, verifying its accuracy along the way.

Bitcoin is the first and most famous blockchain, and it does all those things. It also comes with a currency that can be spent. And that's part of what the Bitcoin blockchain ledger maintains: a tamper-proof record of transactions—who's paying whom.

Now, there are literally thousands of blockchains with varying levels of quality and security. Bitcoin stands out because it's the first, has never been hacked, and has sort of proved to the world the promise of blockchain technology.

Do we know exactly how many cryptocurrencies there are? Or is that hard to pin down?

There are literally thousands of cryptocurrencies. Most of them are kind of fly-by-night hustles that don't have the underlying technology to make them valuable. But since cryptocurrencies attract so many speculators, if you create one, someone out there will be willing to buy it.

What can you tell me about the origins of cryptocurrencies?

They grew out of a movement called cypherpunks, which originated in the 1980s. Cypherpunks were a collection of privacy-obsessed cryptography fans and programmers in the San Francisco Bay Area. These people experimented with how to create a new form of money that didn't rely on a central bank, a government, or other intermediaries.

Their goal came to fruition with the Bitcoin white paper in 2008, which put out this new proof of concept.[1] It's a fundamental theory of a private, decentralized form of money that could not be hacked and did not require trusted authorities to maintain.

So, cryptocurrencies—and bitcoin being the first— are the first application of this blockchain technology.

Yeah. And since it's clear that it does work, it's secure, and it's valuable, people are now building all sorts of other things on top of it. You can think of it as a sort of operating system. And now there are various applications of the technology. Creating currency and spending money is just one.

Who is the person or group behind that 2008 paper— the Benjamin Franklin of the technology, so to speak?

The Benjamin Franklin of Bitcoin and blockchain would be the anonymous author Satoshi [Nakamoto]. It's almost impolite in the world of Bitcoin to speculate on who Satoshi is—but I don't really observe those niceties. I think Satoshi is a mix of those early Bay Area programmers. Namely, a guy named Hal Finney, who died of ALS several years ago, working closely with a guy named Nick Szabo, a polymath programmer, lawyer, and libertarian. And it's pretty clear from the early records and listservs that those two guys, if they're not Satoshi, are indispensable to the success of the project.

So, Satoshi is somewhere between the Benjamin Franklin and Banksy of Bitcoin.

Exactly. Great analogy.

Today, there are billions of dollars of crypto in circulation. It's a huge system. Who governs it?

When you talk to crypto people, the first thing they always tell you is "Decentralized, decentralized, there are no leaders, there's no bank, there's no authority." But every project needs some sort of leaders, for lack of a better word. And even in the case of Bitcoin, which is by far the most decentralized blockchain, there's still a clique of insiders who are responsible for maintaining the code.

Bitcoin is software, and just like your Apple software updates periodically, or your Chrome browser updates, Bitcoin receives updates. Most of them are quite minor, but they'll expand the functionality of it and improve the security of it. There is a core group of developers who are the guardians of Bitcoin. But they don't control it.

Other blockchains are much more centralized. Usually a handful of people control a lot of the money behind it and have an outsized influence. So, decentralization is a spectrum. Bitcoin is the most decentralized—but even it's got influential people who are the guardians of its code. A lot of the newer blockchains are not decentralized at all.

I'm interested in decentralization as it relates to who's able to own and profit from cryptocurrencies. How can we reconcile the concentration of crypto wealth at the moment, when that's really the opposite of the goal of this technology?

There's a term in crypto, "whales," which refers to people who own an outsized amount of bitcoin or ether or something similar. By virtue of owning most of the money, they can have an immense influence on the value of the currency and other governance decisions.

Defenders of crypto would say that whales have a big stake in making it work—it's not in their interest to "pump and dump" it, because then people would lose trust in its value. Although that's the nature of many new blockchains: Spin it up, urge suckers to buy it, then get out. That's been endemic since the early days of crypto.

But the more successful currencies are becoming increasingly decentralized—in the case of Bitcoin and Ethereum especially—in terms of who actually owns the allocations of coins tied to each blockchain.

Switching gears a bit, crypto seems like it will play a huge role in the growth of Web3. Would you say that Web3 is the ecosystem that crypto spawned? Or is it the other way around?

Crypto came first. But what's key to Web3 is having a wallet. MetaMask and Coinbase Wallet (different from a Coinbase account on its centralized exchange) are two of the most popular. Wallets allow you to carry your cryptocurrency around. That's the backbone of Web3. You need money and a wallet, whereas in Web2, you simply need a browser.

Businesses and organizations—how do you see them fitting into this landscape in the future?

I see businesses interacting with Web3 and the crypto world in two ways. One is simply taking payments as more and more people use ether and bitcoin—and increasingly something called stablecoins, which are coins pegged to the U.S. dollar that don't have the same volatility. It's a superior way to move money around. There seems to be a really big push to have everyone, from Wall Street to retailers, switch over to use crypto as a payment mechanism. That's why PayPal and Square (which changed its name to Block to reflect its interest in blockchain) and even Apple are moving in this direction. So I have no doubt that in a few years, crypto is going to be a mainstream payment mechanism.

The other is the more amorphous Web3 world. Should we have a virtual storefront? Should we issue NFTs? Will people interact with our brand in the metaverse? Brands will be asking themselves these kinds of questions. High-fashion brands like Chanel and Gucci are dabbling in this already. But this is all much less proven than crypto.

What are some other businesses using crypto or other Web3 tools in a smart way today?

Again, I'd keep your eye on PayPal, which has facilitated money transfers. And Coinbase, which, of course, is a crypto-native company. They're making a push to challenge the likes of Western Union through international payments and transfers. You're also seeing companies like Robinhood trying to remake stock trading using a more code-based ecosystem to record exchanges and transfers and finance.

I think the more interesting use cases so far are in the arts. In music, there's a lot going on around NFTs to break the conventional record label model. DJ 3LAU and the Chainsmokers are popular musicians deep into NFTs. Gaming, too, is increasingly adopting NFTs. Companies like Ubisoft and Zynga are traditional gaming companies dabbling with them.

Am I right in thinking that crypto is pretty much unregulated, but that's not going to last? If regulations are coming, where are they happening, and what kind of impact do you think they'll have?

Regulation is circling crypto already in many places, and it is moving quickly. The EU has moved seriously to ban

proof-of-work blockchains like Bitcoin due to environmental concerns. China has basically banned crypto altogether. Meanwhile, the U.S. Securities and Exchange
Commission (SEC) is making life difficult for a lot of
crypto startups, and New York passed a bill halting certain types of crypto mining.

The reality is that, contrary to popular imagination, Bitcoin and crypto have always been subject to certain forms
of regulation, especially from law enforcement. But the
pressure from regulators increased dramatically starting
in 2020, as governments have gotten more sophisticated in
their understanding of crypto, and as some countries—
including the United States—have come to view it as an
important new source of tax revenue. This won't stop the
growth of blockchain and Web3, but it will complicate it.

*It can be difficult to understand how digital
currencies could have a real-world, environmental
impact. Could you explain this relationship?*

The environmental impact of crypto is one of the most
misreported and poorly understood subjects when it
comes to crypto discussions. In some cases, it's because
people distrust crypto to begin with. They don't understand it. So they seize on the environmental critique as a
way to project their larger mistrust.

Take Bitcoin, for example. Bitcoin mining—basically, adding blocks to the blockchain—can take a lot of brute-force computing. Once upon a time, you could add a block to the blockchain with your home laptop or with your phone. Now, there are factories devoted to it: warehouses full of servers, going full blast, devoting a massive amount of computing power, which takes a lot of energy to run.

The question becomes, "What kind of energy are you using?" If you're plugged into a hydroelectric dam or solar or wind power, that's not so bad. If you're burning coal, then I think environmentalists have a very good point that this isn't acceptable.

But what's incredibly misunderstood is that Bitcoin is just one part of crypto. It's just one blockchain of many. And the majority of the others rely on much less energy-intensive operations. It's a bit of a red herring when people say, "I'm not touching crypto because of the environmental impact." It depends on which crypto.

I think it's also important to note that the conventional financial system uses a ton of energy, too. So I think Bitcoin proponents object correctly in asking, "Why are we being singled out?"

To close, what are the next steps that need to happen to bring crypto and Web3 into a more mature stage of their life cycles?

The user interface needs to get a lot better. Right now, if you go to prowl around Web3, it's a very clunky experience. In that sense, it's a lot like the early internet before we had browsers. Remember, the internet existed for a long time before the World Wide Web, but we were waiting for the tools to make it accessible to the mainstream.

And on the flip side, what would need to happen for us to look back a couple decades from now and think of crypto as a failed experiment?

I've been writing my crypto for more than 10 years. At this point, I just don't think you can stuff this technology back in the bottle. It's sort of like asking, in 1993, whether the internet's going to be a flop. There's that axiom: We tend to overhype the short-term impact of technology but underestimate the long-term effect of it. I think that absolutely applies to crypto.

. . .

Editor's note: We first interviewed Jeff John Roberts about a month before the May 2022 cryptocurrency crash. We spoke with him again, on May 12, 2022 to ask him about it.

The crypto market has experienced a crash since this article was originally published. Briefly, what's driving it?

The crypto market is being hit by a one-two punch. First, inflation and other macroeconomic forces are driving down the price of assets across the board—and many funds are dumping their crypto holdings first. The other factor is internal to the crypto markets: The collapse of the algorithmic stablecoin terra has led to mass selling of bitcoin and other tokens as people scramble to cover their positions.

Is there a precedent to a crypto market crash of this magnitude?

Believe it or not, yes. There have been spectacular crashes since the very beginning of Bitcoin, notably after a hack of the exchange Mt. Gox in 2014 and the 2020 Covid sell-off. Some of us are joking that this feels like the old days of crypto, when prices regularly swung 30% or 40%.

What might this crash mean for Web3 projects that rely on crypto?

Well, *every* Web3 project relies on crypto, and it's not like a market crash is going to cause blockchain technology to disappear. But obviously a lot of projects are going to have to tighten their belts—and many of the weaker ones that have been propped up by the bubble that just popped will blow away altogether.

As a reporter who has covered this topic for a long time, how do these events change how you think about crypto?

To be honest, these events have mostly confirmed what I thought already: Crypto has been, and remains, highly speculative and volatile. But history shows that the crypto market is cyclical, and it will gradually rebuild and likely surpass its previous highs within a year or two. The only difference this time around is the scale—there are a lot more people losing a lot more money. But the serious entrepreneurs will stay focused on improving their products for the next boom cycle.

TAKEAWAYS

How does cryptocurrency fit into the Web3 ecosystem? Technology journalist Jeff John Roberts explains crypto's popularity and how this momentum is thrusting the public toward Web3.

✓ There are thousands of cryptocurrencies with different levels of security and decentralization. The most common are bitcoin and ether.

✓ While cryptocurrency has been around for years, navigating Web3 effectively will require users to have a crypto wallet to store, receive, or spend cryptocurrencies. Companies are moving toward making crypto a more common payment mechanism.

✓ Cryptocurrency is already more regulated than most think, and further pushes toward regulation are gaining momentum.

✓ Crypto has been criticized for being highly energy-intensive, though its true environmental impact is difficult to measure.

✓ To bring Web3 into the next stage of its maturity, its user interfaces must become more accessible to mainstream users.

NOTES

1. Satoshi Nakamoto, "Bitcoin: A Peer-to-Peer Electronic Cash System," bitcoin.org/bitcoin.pdf.

Adapted from content posted on hbr.org, May 10, 2022 (product #H070U0).

2

WHY BLOCKCHAIN'S ETHICAL STAKES ARE SO HIGH

by Reid Blackman

I f I send you bitcoin, that transaction is simultaneously recorded on the more than 12,000 computers, servers, and other devices that Bitcoin runs on. Everyone on the chain can see the transaction, and no one can alter or delete it. Or you can send me an NFT on the Ethereum blockchain, and that transaction is simultaneously recorded across all the computers (also known as "nodes") that Ethereum runs on. These two examples explain, roughly, what blockchain technology is: a way to keep unalterable records of transactions on multiple computers such that a new transaction cannot be recorded on one computer without simultaneously recording it on all the others. The applications of blockchain have grown well beyond cryptocurrency and NFTs, as governments and industries from health care to agriculture to supply-chain operations leverage the technology to improve efficiency, security, and trust.

The core features of blockchain are tremendously appealing, but they are a double-edged sword, opening novel pathways to significant ethical, reputational, legal, and economic risks for organizations and their stakeholders. Four of these risks are a lack of third-party protections, privacy violations, the zero-state problem, and bad governance. For each, I outline the responsibilities of two actors that play crucial roles in managing blockchain decisions and norms: developers (those who design and develop blockchain technologies and the apps that run on them) and users (the organizations that use blockchain solutions or advise clients who use them).

Lack of Third-Party Protection

Third-party intermediaries, like banks, are often seen as a cost of doing business at best and predatory at worst, but they do play a crucial role in safeguarding customers' interests. For instance, banks have sophisticated ways of detecting activity by malicious actors, and consumers can challenge fraudulent transactions and scams on their credit cards.

When transactions take place without a third party, customers have no one to whom they can appeal for help. This is often the case with blockchain applications. For example, the digital wallets that people and entities use to send and receive digital assets have public keys, akin to publicly listed physical addresses. They also have private keys, which function like passwords and are possessed only by the wallets' owners. Losing a private key is a catastrophic event with no recourse: Owners can no longer access their wallets. In January 2021, the *New York Times* reported that $140 billion worth of bitcoin is locked in wallets whose private keys have been lost or forgotten.[1] With a traditional bank, a lost password delays access to an account only for mere minutes—as opposed to forever.

What developers must consider

Developers need to think about the kinds of services third parties provide that protect stakeholders and then devise a decentralized way to offer those protections. If that is impossible, developers must inform stakeholders that the technology lacks the protections they are accustomed to. A developer may even decide not to develop the app because the risks to users are too high.

What users must consider

Users need to understand the risk of not having those safeguards, for themselves and for those they represent (clients they advise, patients for whom they care, citizens whose rights they are meant to protect). They must be transparent about the risks and get meaningful informed consent from those they serve. They should also explore non-blockchain solutions that can fill in the gaps.

The Lack of Privacy

The most popular blockchains, Bitcoin and Ethereum, are public. Known for their transparency and accessibility, anyone can view, add to, and audit the entirety of the chain. But if transparency constitutes a serious threat to users' privacy, a private blockchain may be necessary. Nebula Genomics, for instance, uses private blockchain technology to give patients "full control" of their genomic data.

A blockchain may contain information that some users should see but not others; in that case, a hybrid approach may be warranted, in which private and public blockchains interact with each other. For example, electronic health records contain both highly sensitive data that must be kept private and information that should be shared with entities such as the Centers for Disease Control and Prevention (CDC) and health insurance providers. Hashed Health, Equideum Health, and BurstIQ are all hybrid blockchains that collect and share biometric information while giving patients more control over their data.

What developers must consider

Developers need to carefully consider their ethical duty to balance transparency and privacy and then decide whether a public, private, or hybrid blockchain is appropriate for the use case at hand. One factor that should loom large is the likelihood that a member of the chain could be identified and what the ethical ramifications of that would be. Other crucial decisions include determining who should have access to what data, under what conditions, and for how long.

What users must consider

Users need to understand the implications of transparency on their own businesses and the people they serve. They must understand and address the risk that wallet holders could be identified (including by their accidentally revealing their own identity).

Suppose the client of a financial services company wants to donate money to a charity or a political party anonymously in order to conceal the size of the donation or to keep political or other affiliations private. The financial services company may recommend transferring the funds via a blockchain because the client's identity will be anonymized on the chain. But it also has an ethical responsibility to inform its client that the anonymous transaction will be public and discuss best practices for avoiding identification.

The Zero-State Problem

The zero-state problem occurs when the accuracy of the data contained in the first, or "genesis block," of a blockchain is in question. This happens if due diligence is not properly performed on the data or if those entering it make a mistake or alter the information for malicious reasons. In the case of a blockchain used to track goods in a supply chain, for example, the first block may erroneously indicate that a particular truck is filled with copper from a certain mine when, in fact, the material came from a different one. Someone involved with the contents of the truck may have been tricked or bribed along the way, unbeknownst to the person creating the genesis block.

The ethical stakes are raised if we're talking about blood diamonds or property. If a government creates a blockchain as the database of record for a land registry, and the person entering information into the first block assigns parcels of land to the wrong owners, a serious injustice (land effectively being stolen) occurs. Some organizations, like Zcash, which created a highly secure privacy-preserving cryptocurrency, have (justifiably) gone to great lengths to ensure the trustworthiness of its genesis block.

What developers must consider

Developers must carefully verify all data that will be contained in the genesis block and use best practices to ensure that it is accurately entered. They must also alert users to the zero-state problem and disclose the ways in which a blockchain may contain false information so that users can assess their potential risks and conduct their own due diligence.

What users must consider

Users of a blockchain should vet how the genesis block was created and where the data was sourced from. They should be particularly diligent if the items recorded in the blockchain have historically been a target for fraud, bribery, and hacking. They should ask themselves, Is the organization that created the first block trustworthy? Has the block been audited by a reliable third party?

Users also need to understand that even if data in the genesis block and subsequent ones is accurate and legitimate, mischief can still occur. For instance, ethically sourced diamonds may be put in a truck, and its journey across multiple transfers may be accurately recorded on the blockchain, but that does not stop clever thieves from swapping out the real diamonds with fake ones mid-transit. Users must also inform those they serve about the zero-state problem, disclose the due diligence they conducted on the genesis block, and identify protections that are in place (if any) to prevent fraud.

Blockchain Governance

Blockchain technology is described by a host of terms—
"decentralized," "permissionless," "self-governed"—that
may cause users to make assumptions about governance.
They might assume that it's a wonderland for libertarians
and anarchists, for example, or that all members have
an equal say in how the blockchain operates. In reality,
blockchain governance is a very, very complicated affair
with significant ethical, reputational, legal, and financial
ramifications. The creators of the blockchain determine
who has power; how they acquire it; what, if any, oversight there is; and how decisions will be made and operationalized. A quick look at two cases, one infamous and
one ongoing, is instructive.

The first DAO, a sort of hedge fund originally called
"The DAO," ran on the Ethereum network. Members had
differing amounts of voting power based on how much
money (specifically, ether) they put into the joint venture. When the DAO was hacked in 2016, draining some
$60 million worth of ether from the fund, members took
very different ideological positions on what to do—and
whether the hack even constituted a "theft." One camp
felt that the ill-gotten gains of the bad actor, who had
taken advantage of a software bug, should be restored

to the rightful owners. Another camp thought The DAO should abstain from undoing the fraudulent transactions and simply fix the bug and let the chain carry on. This group held that "code is law" and "the blockchain is immutable," and thus the hacker, acting in accordance with the code, did nothing ethically unacceptable. The former camp ultimately won, and a "hard fork" was instituted, directing the funds to a recovery address where users could reclaim their investments, essentially rewriting history on the blockchain.

The second example is the dispute about the governance of Juno, another DAO. In February 2021, Juno conducted an "airdrop" (in which free tokens are sent to community members to boost engagement) across its network. One wallet holder figured out how to game the system and received a huge portion of the tokens, worth more than $117 million at the time. In March 2022, a proposal was put forth to draw down the majority of the "whale's" tokens to an amount considered a fair share of the airdrop. A month later, the proposal officially passed, with 72% of the vote, resulting in the revoking of all but 50,000 of the whale's tokens. The whale, who alleges he was investing the money of others, is threatening to sue Juno as of writing.

Those events demonstrate just how important it is to structure the governance of blockchains and the apps that run on blockchains with great care and due diligence.

What developers must consider

Developers must establish what constitutes good governance, with a special eye toward how governance structures can give rise to hacks or bad actors. This is not merely a mechanistic issue. The values of the developers need to be clearly articulated and then operationalized in the blockchain. Consider, for instance, the philosophical differences that emerged as Ethereum developers weighed whether to alter their blockchain when the DAO was hacked or fix the bug and move on, and the similar disagreements between the Juno token holders who voted in favor of confiscation and those who voted against it. To avoid such ethical issues, developers should institute a North Star that guides governance from the start.

Disagreements arise when rules are not carefully thought through about how power and money are allocated or earned on the system. The DAO hacker exploited a bug in the software, which led to internal turmoil about whether code—even flawed code—truly was law. In the case of Juno, the upheaval stemmed, in part, from not being sufficiently thoughtful about how tokens were distributed in the first place. Developers need to understand that those with voting power may have greatly diverging beliefs, values, ideals, and desires. Strong governance is one of the most important tools for managing those differences, and significant ethical and financial risks can be avoided if developers' values are operationalized into the infrastructure, policies, and procedures that govern the blockchain.

What users must consider

Users must ask themselves whether the values of the blockchain's creators cohere with those of their organization and of their clients. They must determine how much volatility, risk, and lack of control they and those they serve can stomach. They must articulate their standards for what constitutes good and responsible governance and work only with blockchains that meet those standards. Users may be using a distributed network with no single authority, but they are most certainly engaging with a political entity.

Toward an Ethical-Risk Framework for Blockchain

The ethical risks of any technology are as varied as the applications for it. An AI-powered self-driving car, for example, carries the risk of killing pedestrians. A social media app comes with the risk of spreading disinformation. The ethical and reputational risks associated with virtually all data-driven technology also apply to blockchain. In implementing blockchain, senior leaders must implement a framework for mitigating these risks. They should carefully consider a range of scenarios: What are the ethical nightmares our organization must avoid? How do we think about the edge cases? They should anticipate that ethical questions will arise, and ask themselves: What governance structures do we have in place? What kind of oversight is needed? Is blockchain technology likely to undermine any of our organizational and ethical values, and if so, how do we minimize those impacts? What protections should be put in place to safeguard our stakeholders and our brand? Thankfully, many of these issues have been addressed in the adjacent AI ethical-risk literature. This material is a good starting point for any blockchain project.

. . .

The Wild West promised limitless opportunity for those bold enough to venture into a new land. But there's a reason the term became synonymous with lawlessness and peril. The world of blockchain is both a game changer and uncharted territory, and senior leaders charged with protecting their corporate brand from ethical, reputational, legal, and economic harm had better pay careful attention to what they do in this world and with whom they do it.

TAKEAWAYS

Blockchain may expose organizations to new kinds of ethical, reputational, legal, and economic risks. There are four specific types of risks that both developers and users should examine.

✓ Lack of third-party protection. Developers must think about services third parties provide that protect stakeholders and devise a decentralized way to offer those protections. Users must understand the risk of not having those safeguards.

✓ Lack of privacy. Developers must consider their ethical duty to balance transparency and privacy and decide whether a public, private, or hybrid blockchain is appropriate. Users must understand the implications of transparency on their own businesses and customers.

✓ Zero-state problems. Developers must ensure the accuracy of the data contained in foundational "genesis" block of each blockchain. Users should vet how the genesis block was created and where the data was sourced from.

✓ Blockchain governance. Developers must establish good governance and ensure governance structures cannot give rise to hacks or bad actors. Users must ask themselves whether the values of the blockchain's creators cohere with those of their organization and their clients.

NOTES

1. Nathaniel Popper, "Lost Passwords Lock Millionaires Out of Their Bitcoin Fortunes," *New York Times*, January 12, 2021, https://www.nytimes.com/2021/01/12/technology/bitcoin-passwords-wallets-fortunes.html.

Adapted from content posted on hbr.org, May 10, 2022 (product #H070TT).

3

WHAT A DAO CAN—AND CAN'T—DO

by Jonathan Ruane and Andrew McAfee

I n November 2021, a group of individuals formed a legal entity that bought 40 acres of land in Wyoming. This kind of thing happens all the time, of course. But the closer we look at this particular real estate transaction, the stranger it becomes.

The purchasing group included approximately 6,000 people. They met via online discussion platforms such as Discord and bought the land not with dollars, yen, or any other fiat currency, but instead with cryptocurrency. It's not clear exactly *what* they bought: Individuals' legal claims on the land itself and the proceeds from its use or sale are not yet, as of writing, settled.

But the strangest part of this deal is that no one runs the entity that purchased the land—it doesn't have a CEO, a board of directors, managers, or other decision-makers. No people at all were involved. The group votes to make decisions, but this process happens automatically, triggering important activities like releasing the money to purchase the land. And the vote is truly binding: No one person has the ability, let alone the authority, to overturn it. Human intervention isn't required or even possible.

Confused? Welcome to the world of DAOs.

Introduction to DAOs

DAO (pronounced as "Dow," like the Dow Jones Industrial Average) is the acronym for *decentralized autonomous organization*. A DAO is a new type of digital-first entity that shares similarities with a traditional company structure but has some additional features, such as the automatic enforcement of operating rules via smart contracts (we'll explain more about these and why they are so interesting). DAOs come in many structures, but all operate as collectives in which members make decisions democratically. No single person exerts control in the way a conventional CEO or senior management team would.

Like most other Web3 technologies, DAOs are currently in an experimental phase. The forms, structures, legalities, and use cases are all still emergent. While the United States has seen tens of millions of corporations registered over the past two centuries, there are fewer than 5,000 DAOs worldwide today according to industry-tracking site DeepDAO, and fewer than 100 have assets of more than $1 million. DAOs attract interest not because of their current scale but because of the novel activities they're undertaking: making investments, establishing new kinds of communities, acquiring items of historical or cultural importance, and engaging in philanthropy.

How DAOs Are Built

DAOs are often formed by congregations of strangers who are geographically dispersed but share a common goal. It's not unusual for individuals to float the initial ideas on platforms such as Twitter or Discord first; if there's enough appeal, others join the online conversations, as they would on a traditional messaging board or in a chat room. DAOs have formed to collect digital artwork, raise funds for the Ukrainian military, distribute grants to fund biotech research, and even try to buy an NBA franchise.

Taking a concept from the initial idea to a functioning DAO requires a group of developers to create a set of smart contracts that form the DAO's core operating system. Smart contracts are self-executing computer programs used to enact decisions by establishing principles such as voting mechanisms (more on these later). These programs can also complete a trade such as moving a digital currency like bitcoin from one wallet to another without human involvement.

These contracts-as-code automatically go into effect once certain criteria have been met. They always perform as written, with no room for misinterpretation (although they don't always perform as *intended*, given the potential for human coding error). Getting these codified rules correct from the outset is important. Even small errors or omissions can cause large headaches and operational failures later on, such as security vulnerabilities that allow hackers to siphon off money.

Once the DAO has established a core set of rules and embedded them into smart contracts, it needs to raise funds. DAOs typically raise funds by issuing tokens, a form of digital currency tied to the smart contract. Sales happen through public or private offerings, and the money raised goes to the DAO's treasury. The tokens represent a form of ownership but are not the same as traditional equity and do not function as investment contracts; rather, they are akin to contributions that bestow governance rights but not ownership. Most DAOs are not directly owned by anyone in the traditional sense.

After the DAO completes the funding phase and becomes operational on blockchain, its original creators have no more influence on the project than any other stakeholder. From this point on, decisions are made by all of the members, who must reach a consensus on proposals, and no central authority exists in the way senior managers or directors run a company.

DAOs in Practice

Typically, token owners put forward proposals about the DAO's operations, then the community votes on each idea. It's not unusual for a lot of discussion and ideation to occur around these proposals on messaging platforms such as Discord. If the final vote is in favor of the proposal, the smart contract will enforce the activity.

Voting procedures differ between DAOs, ranging from simple majority to quadratic voting (in which a person gets an allocation of votes and can place more than one vote for a proposal they strongly support). Information related to issues such as currency transactions and internal decisions is available for everyone to see on blockchain. This transparency forms the basis for trust among members.

An important feature of this process is that voting mechanisms are defined in advance and not easily modified. This differs from what happens in traditional organizations, where a CEO or CFO can ignore consensus when making a decision. In a DAO, the community votes on activities such as spending money. Although the scope of decisions that can be made this way is more limited than in a traditional organization, once everyone agrees to the rules, there's no ambiguity or wiggle room in how they are applied.

Adhering to smart contract-enforced decisions means a DAO is less suited to commercial situations with more ambiguity or those in which success comes from organizational dynamism—the ability to adapt to subtle changes in market conditions, including the early stages of markets being formed for innovative products or services. During this period, entrepreneurs must make judgments using incomplete data and iterate at speed; writing detailed smart contracts to support this work would be difficult, if not impossible.

That said, communities are forming DAOs around a wide range of concepts, including investments, management of other blockchain-based projects, and content production. Most people putting money into DAOs understand that they might not see this investment again. They are usually participating in a pet project with funds they can afford to lose, not unlike backing a Kickstarter project. To support the development process, new firms are springing up to empower those wishing to create DAOs by simplifying technical processes, removing friction points, and providing templates and tools. The startup Upstream, for example, offers a "no-code, full-stack platform," supplying tools that it claims will enable anyone to start and run a DAO.

The Limits of DAOs

As an emergent form of commercial organization, DAOs are not yet fully accounted for in a legal sense, and many are pushing traditional boundaries. For most jurisdictions there are questions around issues such as how a DAO should file and pay taxes or sign legally binding contracts. The majority of existing DAOs are unregistered and have an uncertain legal status, and they are perhaps viewed as "alegal" rather than illegal. This uncertainty could be detrimental to the development of DAOs, but conforming to existing rules is also difficult. The very nature of a decentralized organization means there's no need for officers and directors, but these are important roles within corporations, especially when things go awry. The transnational membership base of DAOs adds to the legal complexity of these groups.

Knowing who you are dealing with is an important foundation for most economic activity as well. This foundation makes it possible for an entity to sue or be sued and to enter into contractual agreements, as well as to acquire, hold, develop, and dispose of property rights. Traditional corporations meet this identifiability standard and have long been recognized as "right-and-duty bearing units"—meaning they are the subjects of rights and liabilities as defined by the legal system in which they operate. Most jurisdictions around the world require a company to provide a unique name, a physical office address, and the name of at least one director in order for the company to receive its own identification number and be entered into the formal business register.

These requirements are challenging for DAOs to meet, especially because many participants operate on the basis of pseudonymity. But what's happening in Wyoming may be motivation for DAOs wishing to formalize their relationship with legal institutions and interact with a jurisdiction on a more solid footing.

CityDAO: A Peek at the Future?

In July 2021, Wyoming became the first state in the United States to explicitly codify rules around DAOs wishing to become domiciled in that jurisdiction. This rule change means that DAOs in Wyoming are considered a distinct form of limited liability company, which grants them a legal personality and confers a wide range of rights, such as limited liability for members. Without this protection, a DAO could be viewed as a general partnership, exposing its members to personal liability for any of the DAO's obligations or actions. Each DAO must have a registered agent in Wyoming, and the agent must establish a physical address and maintain a register of names and addresses of the entity's directors or individuals serving in a similar capacity.

One of the first entities established after this legislation was born as an idea in a tweet by Scott Fitsimones. A small group of founding citizens from countries including Germany, the United States, Ireland, and Canada then came together to create CityDAO in July 2021 with the objective of "building the city of the future on the Ethereum blockchain." To do this, the group would need to decentralize asset ownership by tokenizing land, rights, and governance. Since CityDAO's founding, the aforementioned approximately 6,000 investors have joined them, contributing nearly $7 million.

CityDAO's first investment (named Parcel 0) was the 40-acre plot of land in Wyoming. This purchase was seen as low-risk by the members and as a first step CityDAO could take as it experimented and figured things out moving forward.

For now, CityDAO citizens get an NFT, which is a digital asset without a direct share in the ownership of real-world land. The NFT strictly represents governance rights (proposing and voting on activities). Members can vote on what the DAO should do, but they don't have a direct return on those activities in the form of anticipated earnings. This arrangement is intended to help ensure that the DAO and its members don't run afoul of federal securities laws. When ownership comes with a reason-able expectation of profits to be derived from the efforts of others (part of what is known as the *Howey* test), the U.S. SEC views the activity as an investment contract and requires strict standards to be met, including registration of the security and detailed information disclosure. All of this might change in the future, but such rules remain a challenge for most DAOs today.

Members of CityDAO see their activities as very much in the experimental phase at this time. They are willing to figure out potential futures through trial and error. Going forward, communication and collaboration will be important for the group to achieve its broad-based objective of "building the city of the future." To enable the sharing of information, members voted to give $24,000 to one of their own, Eric Gilbert-Williams, to produce *CityDAO Podcast*, which features leaders in the community discussing topics related to CityDAO.

Although the Wyoming legislation moves the legal status of DAOs forward in that state, uncertainties remain around tax treatment, legal standing outside Wyoming, the nuances of applying securities laws to tokens, and other issues.

It's unlikely that DAOs will replace traditional organizations, or at least they won't anytime soon. But their current shortcomings should be viewed through the lens of early-stage innovation: It's not clear exactly what they will become and where they are most beneficial, but DAOs have obviously created a lot of interest and excitement in the Web3 community. Will DAOs take the place of traditional organizations for some types of group-level activity? Will we see hybrids form, where, for example, "normal" companies use smart contracts to make ironclad, irrevocable commitments to a constituency? Imagine using something like a DAO to let your employees vote on which philanthropies to support or users decide which features to incorporate in the next version of an offering. With Web3, there's plenty to imagine.

A DAO—decentralized autonomous organization—is a digital-first entity that shares qualities with a traditional company structure but has some additional features, such as the automatic enforcement of operating rules via smart contracts. They are often formed by geographically dispersed strangers based on a common goal they all share.

✓ DAOs can vary in forms, structures, legalities, and use, but they may make and spend money, invest in other entities, establish new kinds of communities, acquire items of historical or cultural importance, or engage in philanthropy.

✓ Smart contracts form DAOs' core operating systems, establishing principles for voting mechanisms, trades, and general rules.

✓ In a legal sense, DAOs are not fully accounted for; they are "alegal" due to their decentralized nature, which allows them to push traditional boundaries commercial organizations cannot.

✓ The forms and structures of DAOs are still in an experimental phase, and it remains unclear whether, and how, DAOs might supplant traditional organizational structures.

Adapted from content posted on hbr.org, May 10, 2022 (product #H070U3).

WHY BUILD IN WEB3

by Jad Esber and Scott Duke Kominers

oday's dominant internet platforms are built on aggregating users and user data. As these platforms have grown, so has their ability to provide value—thanks to the power of network effects—which has enabled them to stay ahead. For example, Facebook's (now Meta's) data on user behavior helped it fine-tune its algorithms to a point that its content feed and ad targeting were dramatically better than what competitors could offer. Amazon, meanwhile, has exploited its broad view into customer demand to both optimize delivery logistics and develop its own product lines. And YouTube has built a massive library of videos from a wide array of creators, enabling it to offer viewers content on almost any topic.

In these business models, locking in users and their data is a key source of competitive advantage. As a result, traditional internet platforms typically do not share data even in aggregate—and they make it difficult for users to export their social graphs and other content. So, even if users grow dissatisfied with a given platform, it's often not worth it to leave.

But all of this might be changing. While it's hard for newcomers to challenge "Web 2.0" companies like Meta on their own terms, now companies—working in what they're calling a "Web3" model—are proposing a novel value proposition. Despite all the public conversations around the metaverse and various hyper-financialized NFT projects, Web3, more than anything, is a fundamentally different approach that some developers have agreed to. It's based on the premise that there's an alternative to exploiting users for data to make money—and that instead, building open platforms that share value with users directly will create more value for everyone, including the platform.

In Web3, instead of platforms having full control of the underlying data, users typically own whatever content they have created (such as posts or videos), as well as digital objects they have purchased. Moreover, these digital assets are typically created according to interoperable standards on public blockchains, instead of being privately hosted on a company's servers. This makes the assets "portable," in the sense that a user can, in principle, leave any given platform whenever they want by unplugging from that app and moving—along with their data—to another one.

This is a major shift, which could fundamentally change how digital companies operate: Users' ability to take their data from one platform to another introduces new sources of competitive pressure, and likely requires firms to update their business strategies. If a platform isn't creating enough value for its users, they might simply leave. And indeed, in Web3, new entrants can explicitly incentivize power users to move to them—for instance, the NFT trading platform LooksRare recently launched through what's called a "vampire attack," a Web3 phenomenon in which one platform "sucks" participants away from another platform, rewarding people for switching over from the dominant platform OpenSea.

But at the same time, the dynamics of Web3 are less zero-sum, which means a platform's overall value creation opportunity can be bigger. Building on an interoperable infrastructure layer makes it easy for platforms to plug into broader content networks, thereby expanding the scale and types of value they can provide their users. A Web3 art gallery, for example, can bootstrap off the artwork users have already created on the blockchain, rather than requiring them to upload art to the platform directly.

This can be a valuable approach to sourcing content even for established platforms. Twitter recently introduced a feature whereby users can show NFTs they own in their profiles; Instagram is working on something similar. And for new platforms, the ability to integrate preexisting digital assets can be critical in resolving what's called the "cold-start problem"—the reality that it can be challenging for a platform to get momentum early on because of a lack of initial content.

Moreover, the infrastructure layer means that the costs associated with creating user trust are much lower in Web3. Managing digital assets on public ledgers makes it clearer which assets exist and who owns what, which was previously a struggle on the web. If a digital artist, for example, claims that a new artwork is limited to 489 editions, then prospective owners can verify that on the blockchain directly—without needing to trust the artist themself, or having a gallery or other intermediary provide such an assurance.

This trust framework extends to the software that runs Web3 platforms: key operations can be encoded on the blockchain in "smart contracts" that are auditable and immutable. This makes it possible for a platform designer to commit up front to certain design features, such as pricing rules, royalty agreements, and user reward mechanics.

All of this means that—at least in theory—it can be much easier to launch a product in Web3. Even an unknown entrepreneur can build products that plug into an existing network without permission from an established platform. Indeed, taken to the limit, in Web3, users sometimes have no need to trust the company (or people) behind a project; rather, they just have to trust the code itself. Some fundraising campaigns supporting humanitarian aid efforts in Ukraine, for example, were run through smart contracts that automatically transfer all funds received to the Ukrainian government or associated charities; this means donors can trust that their funds will be used properly even if the campaign organizers are completely anonymous.

Of course, given the early financial use cases of Web3 and the high volume of transactions, a number of bad actors have leveraged the hype to orchestrate scams. Many of the Web3 experiences today were designed for tech-savvy power users, whereas ordinary users might have only a limited understanding of what an app or platform can actually do, much less be able to vet source code to verify that it functions as described. There's a long way to go before Web3 technology is safe and accessible to the average consumer.

Furthermore, plugging into an existing network in practice doesn't mean you can automatically unlock an engaged user base that wants to stick around. Just as in all entrepreneurial ventures, it's essential to build a product that solves for a true user need. But once you *have* solved a user need, leveraging established networks through Web3 makes it much easier to deploy and scale.

Making platform backends open and interoperable enables compounding innovation and incentivizes direct investment in building the infrastructure layers. For example, koodos—a Web3 service that lets people create collections of things they love from across the internet—is building shared infrastructure that any network can plug into and improve. (Disclosure: Esber cofounded koodos, and Kominers provides market design advice to the company.)

Sharing infrastructure means that apps can focus on building great experiences, driving toward a greater emphasis on platform design as a source of competitive advantage. What an app has understood about its market manifests in its user experience and interface—and so even in Web3, the insights consumer apps generate about their users will continue to differentiate them.

Web3 platforms also have the potential to unlock a novel and especially powerful form of network effect through community engagement and social cohesion.

Ownership of digital assets fosters a sense of psychological ownership that can make consumers feel so invested in a product that it becomes almost an extension of themselves. A platform's users literally become "fans" who form a bond through the shared platform experience—similar to how fans of a sports team or obscure band see themselves as a community.

For example, The Hundreds, a popular streetwear brand, sold NFTs themed around its mascot, the "Adam Bomb." Holding one of these NFTs gives access to community events and exclusive merchandise, providing a way for the brand's fans to meet and engage with each other—and thus reinforcing their enthusiasm. The Hundreds also spontaneously announced that it would pay royalties (in store credit) to owners of the NFTs associated with Adam Bombs that were used in some of its clothing collections. This made it roughly as if you could have part ownership in the Ralph Lauren emblem, and every new line of polos that used that emblem would give you a dividend. Partially decentralizing the brand's value in this way led everyone in The Hundreds's community to feel even more attached to the IP and to go out of their way to promote it—to the point that some community members even got Adam Bomb tattoos.

Another example is SushiSwap, which is a "fork" of the decentralized finance platform Uniswap—meaning

SushiSwap's underlying algorithms are a clone of the code that Uniswap published. The main difference is that SushiSwap set up a strong brand and community, alongside an active and ongoing reward system for users that drove higher user engagement and positive sentiment about the platform; this then enabled it to quickly emerge as a successful competitor to Uniswap.

More generally, sharing ownership allows for more incentive alignment between products and their derivatives, creating incentives for everyone to become a builder and contributor. The underlying technology standards also enable every Web3 company to be built upon. This means the community around a platform can co-create in a way that's much less adversarial than in the past and with more derivatives in circulation—making the platform ecosystem grow even stronger.

In the short run, this model gives up some share of consumer surplus to the builder or creator. But because the builders get more, they're strongly incentivized to invest and grow the total pie for everyone, which means that in the long run, Web3 should raise consumer surplus as well.

. . .

Web3 has the potential to unlock a more valuable internet for everyone. New companies can build on Web3 infrastructure to create communities around their brands and product concepts much more easily than in previous iterations of the web. And even established platforms can leverage these forces by plugging into blockchain-based content networks and giving their users some ownership over their data. All of this means that the next era of the web will likely look a lot different—and more open—than the one we're living with today.

TAKEAWAYS

Today's dominant internet platforms have guarded their troves of user data and maintained an advantage through network effects. Companies using Web3 have a new value proposition for users.

- ✓ In Web3, users—not platforms—own whatever content they have created, as well as digital objects they have purchased, and these digital assets are typically portable.

- ✓ This new paradigm makes it easier for new companies to compete with established ones if they offer better user experience.

✓ Because the system is less zero-sum than Web2, user lock-in isn't the primary goal for platforms. A platform's overall value creation opportunity can be bigger.

✓ The costs associated with creating user trust are much lower in Web3. Managing digital assets on public ledgers makes it clearer which assets exist and who owns what.

✓ These features taken together may mean that it will be easier to launch a product in Web3—users just have to trust a project's code, not necessarily the company or people behind it.

Adapted from content posted on hbr.org, May 16, 2022 (product #H0713Z)

5

HOW BRANDS ARE EXPERIMENTING WITH WEB3

by Ana Andjelic

E arly Web3 initiatives mark both a technological advancement and a new approach to corporate strategy. Early adopters of these tools are using them to get a better understanding of consumer behavior so that they can more accurately—and competitively—chart customer journeys and participate in customer communities. These efforts help build companies' brands and power transparency around supply, production, and distribution, boosting corporate governance and sustainability credentials.

In this article, I examine how three different approaches to Web3—virtual products, hybrid products, and decentralized ownership—can deliver immediate business value. By experimenting with each, brands can take advantage of this new era of the internet to amplify and diversify their digital footprint.

Virtual Products

Many brands are creating their own Web3 products, often in partnership with established producers of and platforms for virtual assets. Think NFTs, Roblox avatars, *Fortnite* skins, or property in Decentraland. Companies retain full control over the assets they create, including how they look and work in virtual environments and digital wallets. These experiments both attract the attention of younger audiences and yield useful insights on their behavior.

Kering, the luxury holding company, has a team dedicated to Web3, and its brands Gucci and Balenciaga have unveiled several metaverse initiatives. For example, the "Gucci Garden" experience, a collaboration with Roblox, was a promotional virtual environment that people could explore with their avatars for two weeks in May 2021. As part of the event, a digital version of the real-world

Gucci bag sold for 350,000 Robux (the cryptocurrency of Roblox), which is $4,115 in real-world money. Ralph Lauren partnered with Roblox in December 2021 to sell virtual winter sportswear that avatars can try on in stores in that virtual world; the company credited its strong earnings for the quarter in part to the campaign and associated investments.

One downside of selling digital products is their limited applicability outside their platforms of origin. Those virtual Ralph Lauren coats, for example, can be worn only in Roblox, not in *Fortnite* or other digital spaces. The virtual properties built in Decentraland, like fashion brand Philipp Plein's building complex, exist only within it. The lack of interoperability between Web3 platforms is an obstacle to greater customer adoption and to greater utility of brand-generated tokens and properties. Another challenge is monetization of Web3 assets. Artifacts like NFTs and game skins are still mostly regarded as marketing and PR experiments and sit outside a company's production, design, and merchandising functions.

Near term, the biggest potential of digital products is in customer intelligence. These assets, which are cheaper to produce than physical goods, can be used to quickly gauge the appeal of a product aesthetic or design, and companies can then turn the most popular virtual items into physical ones.

Hybrid Products

Another way companies are using Web3 is to enrich their real-world products with digital information. Here's how it works: First, information about a product is recorded on the blockchain in the form of a smart contract, or transaction protocols that automatically execute legally relevant events and actions according to set terms. Data recorded might include the product's origin, supply, production, and design, and once recorded on the blockchain, this information is immutable. The physical item thus becomes a collectible because of its uniqueness and authenticity. This allows brands to prevent counterfeiting and to benefit from secondary sales, which has traditionally been difficult to do.

For example, the National Basketball Association's Top Shot store sells video highlights of especially compelling shots—like a clutch three-pointer from Warriors star Steph Curry—as collectible NFT "trading cards." Created by Dapper Labs, a blockchain company, in partnership with the NBA and its players' union in 2020, these virtual trading cards include not only the highlight clip but also team-specific artwork, game and player stats, a description of the action, a unique serial number, and additional details.

Other examples show the varied ways firms are experimenting with hybrid products. The entertainment company Secret Level creates NFTs of classic TV and film scenes (in conjunction with the content's creators) that fans can buy, collect, and trade via blockchain. Clothing company Anybodies has a line of NFTs that owners can sell, share, or redeem for its limited-edition hoodies. Coach, the luxury fashion brand, launched an NFT collection for the 2021 holidays, giving buyers a special bag that wasn't available otherwise. Companies can even, as Adidas has done, record attendance at virtual or real-world events, like a fashion show or a collection launch, on the blockchain and reward the people who came with preferential access to new products and sales, exclusive invites to other events, and personal styling services.

The benefits brands accrue from the hybrid approach are twofold: One is verifiable information on products' origins; the second is community-building. Downsides, however, include the energy and environmental costs of creating tokens and recording information on the blockchain. In the United States, bitcoin mining—the process of creating new bitcoins by solving math problems that verify transactions in the currency—creates an estimated 40 billion pounds of carbon emissions, according to *Business Insider*.[1]

In addition, to produce and manage these products, you need talent well versed in cryptocurrency and the blockchain; interdepartmental collaboration, with marketing, production, merchandising, and technology all coming together to develop successful hybrids; and state-of-the-art customer-relationship-management programs so that actions can be recorded on the blockchain and rewarded.

Distributed Ownership

Distributed ownership is a new brand-governance paradigm. Instead of a company selling one item to one customer, this strategy is about multiple customers sharing ownership of something via the blockchain. While I'm not aware of any traditional brands using this strategy, digital-first companies are. As the technology evolves and experimentation continues, all marketers should understand how distributed ownership works, since it has the potential to change the way customer communities are managed—and how product value is created and shared.

For example, Otis is a distributed ownership platform where users buy, sell, and trade SEC-securitized shares of collectibles like artworks, comics, jewelry, or fashion clothing items, thus building portfolios of alternative assets. If a consumer wants to invest in the sneakers that Michael Jordan was wearing when his dunk shattered the backboard glass in a 1985 game, for example, they could purchase a small share of the shoes through Otis or a similar platform. The consumer can then earn a return either if they sell their share or if the group of shareowners collectively decides to sell the sneakers.

There are a few scenarios for how this type of governance could play out for legacy brands. The first is a shared shopping cart. In this scenario, there are two item prices: one for individual buying and another for the shared shopping cart. When buyers select the latter, they join a group in which they can negotiate for lower prices and get discounts. A shared shopping cart is suitable for mass-market brands; it is already used by the Chinese marketplace Pinduoduo.

In the second scenario, midrange and premium brands can encourage group buying, which gives them real-time information about customer demand. This real-time information is based on individual purchase patterns and browsing histories, but also on the purchase patterns and browsing histories of everyone in the buying group. That information, in turn, allows brands to negotiate more-favorable rates with manufacturers. The results are better prices for consumers and less risk that companies will need to offload excess inventory (and devalue their brand).

In the third scenario, for luxury brands, buyers gain shared ownership of a particularly valuable item, like a handbag or a piece of jewelry, that is either passed along through the group or treated like an investment to be later resold at a profit.

At scale, a distributed ownership platform might look like Friends with Benefits, a self-described "headless media community lifestyle brand" network, in which members have different levels of access and governing power depending how many tokens they've earned or bought on the collectively owned platform. Perks of membership range from an FWB newsletter subscription to FWB Discord channel access to tickets for in-person events, all aimed at forging connections, creating project teams, or pursuing joint investments. FWB is fully user-led and has become everything from a music discovery platform to a startup incubator to a meeting place for crypto investors. Fee-paying members jointly agree on the purchases and investments the network makes, and all actions are recorded on the Ethereum blockchain.

Brands benefit from distributed ownership because it generates returns on production and property rights, while consumers get tangible rewards and partial ownership. With increased market activity, the value of the token or product increases and, in return, attracts more participants that generate even more activity. It's a virtuous cycle.

That said, when there is little or no demand, that positive feedback loop between product or token value and market activity doesn't exist. Another risk brands face in offering decentralized ownership is lack of control. Successful decentralized platforms are still, in most cases, more proposal than reality.

. . .

The technology behind all these Web3 approaches remains nascent. But as brands better understand the opportunities and challenges and refine their approaches, their early experiments could turn into ongoing strategy.

TAKEAWAYS

Web3 could be a "winners-share-all" model, where products, services, markets, and exchanges are built together, governed together, and benefit together. Brands are experimenting with three main approaches to connecting with customers and creating value with Web3. Each carries benefits and pitfalls.

✓ Virtual products can be created in partnership with established virtual asset producers. These experiments both attract the attention of certain audiences and yield useful insights on their behavior. Unfortunately, these products cannot be used outside their platform of origin.

✓ Hybrid products allow companies to enrich real-world products with immutable digital information on a blockchain that makes it resistant to counterfeiting, but this approach adds to the product's carbon footprint.

✓ Distributed ownership can create new kinds of customer communities. Digital-first companies are experimenting with giving members different levels of access, governing power, perks, and monetary returns based on their tokens in a platform.

NOTES

1. Paul Kim, "What Are the Environmental Impacts of Cryptocurrencies?," *Business Insider*, March 17, 2022, https://www.businessinsider.com/personal-finance/cryptocurrency-environmental-impact.

Adapted from content posted on hbr.org, May 10, 2022 (product #H070U6).

6

CAUTIONARY TALES FROM CRYPTOLAND

An interview with Molly White by
Thomas Stackpole

A s the hype around Web3 has reached a fever pitch, critics have started to warn of unintended and over-looked consequences of a web with a blockchain backbone. And while Web3 advocates focus on what the future of the internet *could* be, skeptics such as Molly White, a software developer and Wikipedia editor, are focused on the very real problems of the here and now.

White created the website Web3 Is Going Just Great, a timeline that tracks scams, hacks, rug pulls, collapses, shady dealings, and other examples of problems with

Web3. HBR.org's tech editor Tom Stackpole spoke to White over email about what people aren't hearing about Web3, how blockchain could make internet harassment much worse, and why the whole project might be, as the site's tagline puts it, "an enormous grift that's pouring lighter fluid on our already smoldering planet." This interview has been lightly edited.

HBR: *You make it very clear that you don't have a financial stake in Web3 one way or another. So what led you to start your project and write about Web3's problems?*

MOLLY WHITE: Late 2021 was when I really began to notice a huge shift in how people talk about crypto. Instead of being primarily used for speculative investments by people who were willing to take on a lot of risk in exchange for hopes of huge returns, people began to talk about how the whole web was going to shift toward services that were built using blockchains. Everyone would have a crypto wallet, and everyone would adopt these new blockchain-based projects for social networks, video games, online communities, and so on.

This shift got my attention, because until then crypto had always felt fairly "opt-in" to me. It was previously a somewhat niche technology, even to software engineers, and it seemed like the majority of people who engaged with it financially were fairly aware of the volatility risks. Those of us who didn't want anything to do with crypto could just not put any money into it.

Once crypto began to be marketed as something that everyone would need to engage with, and once projects began trying to bring in broader, more mainstream audiences—often people who didn't seem to understand the technology or the financial risks—I got very concerned. Blockchains are not well suited to many, if not most, of the use cases that are being described as "Web3," and I have a lot of concerns about the implications of them being used in that way. I also saw just an enormous number of crypto and Web3 projects going terribly: people coming up with incredibly poorly thought-out project ideas and people and companies alike losing tons of money to scams, hacks, and user error.

In the examples you've collected, what are some of the common mistakes or misapprehensions you see in companies' efforts to launch Web3 projects, whether they're NFTs or something else?

My overwhelming feeling is that Web3 projects seem to be a solution in search of a problem. It often seems like project creators knew they wanted to incorporate block-chains somehow and then went casting around for some problem they could try to solve with a blockchain without much thought as to whether it was the right technology to address it, or even if the problem was something that could or should be solved with technology at all.

Kickstarter might have been the most egregious example of this: Late in 2021 it announced, much to the chagrin of many in its user base, that it would be completely rebuilding its platform on a blockchain. A few months later, in an interview to explain the decision, COO Sean Leow gave the distinct impression that he had no idea why Kickstarter was reimplementing its platform this way—what governance problems it was trying to solve, why a blockchain would be effective in solving them.[1]

Companies also seem to announce NFT projects without doing much research into how these have gone for other companies in their sector. We've seen enough NFT announcements by video game studios that have gone so badly that they've chosen to reverse the decision within days or even hours. And yet somehow a new game company will do this and then be surprised at the backlash over NFTs' considerable carbon footprint or the sense that they're just a grift. The same is true for ostensibly environmentally conscious organizations announcing NFTs—even in some cases projects that are entirely focused on environmentalism, like the World Wildlife Fund, which tried and failed to launch a less carbon-intensive NFT series.

I firmly believe that companies first need to identify and research the problem they are trying to solve, and *then* select the right technology to do it. Those technologies may not be the latest buzzword, and they may not cause venture capitalists to come crawling out of the woodwork, but choosing technologies with that approach tends to be a lot more successful in the long run—at least, assuming the primary goal is to actually solve a problem rather than attract VC money.

One of the most surprising (to me, anyway) arguments you make is that Web3 could be a disaster for privacy and create major issues around harassment. Why? And does it feel like the companies "buying into" Web3 are aware of this?

Blockchains are immutable, which means once data is recorded, it can't be removed. The idea that blockchains will be used to store user-generated data for services like social networks has enormous implications for user safety. If someone uses these platforms to harass and abuse others, such as by doxing, posting revenge pornography, uploading child sexual abuse material, or doing any number of other very serious things that platforms normally try to thwart with content-moderation teams, the protections that can be offered to users are extremely limited. The same goes for users who plagiarize artwork, spam, or share sensitive material like trade secrets. Even a user who themself posts something and then later decides they'd rather not have it online is stuck with it remaining on-chain indefinitely.

Many blockchains also have a very public record of transactions: Anyone can see that a person made a transaction and the details of that transaction. Privacy is theoretically provided through pseudonymity—wallets are identified by a string of characters that aren't inherently tied to a person. But because you'll likely use one wallet for most of your transactions, keeping one's wallet address private can be both challenging and a lot of work and is likely to only become more challenging if this future vision of crypto ubiquity is realized. If a person's wallet address is known and they are using a popular chain like Ethereum to transact, anyone [else] can see all transactions they've made.

Imagine if you went on a first date, and when you paid them back for your half of the meal, they could now see every other transaction you'd ever made—not just the public transactions on some app you used to transfer the cash but *any* transactions: the split checks with all of your previous dates, that monthly transfer to your therapist, the debts you're paying off (or not), the charities to which you're donating (or not), the amount you're putting in a retirement account (or not). What if they could see the location of the corner store by your apartment where you so frequently go to grab a pint of ice cream at 10 p.m.? And this would also be visible to your ex-partners, your estranged family members, your prospective employers, or any number of outside parties interested in collecting your data and using it for any purpose they like. If you had a stalker or had left an abusive relationship or were the target of harassment, the granular details of your life are right there.

There are some blockchains that try to obfuscate these types of details for privacy purposes. But there are trade-offs here: While transparency can enable harassment, the features that make it possible to achieve privacy in a trustless system also enable financial crimes like money laundering. It is also very difficult to use those currencies (and to cash them out to traditional forms of currency). There are various techniques that people can use to try to remain anonymous, but they tend to require technical skill and quite a lot of work on the user's end to maintain that anonymity.

This point of view seems almost totally absent from the conversation. Why do you think that is?

I think a lot of companies haven't put much thought into the technology's abuse potential. I'm surprised at how often I bring it up and the person I'm talking to admits that it's never crossed their mind.

When the abuse potential is acknowledged, there's a very common sentiment in the Web3 space that these fundamental problems are just minor issues that can be fixed later, without any acknowledgment that they are intrinsic characteristics of the technology that can't easily be changed after the fact. I believe it's completely unacceptable to release products without any apparent thought to this vector of user risk, and so I am shocked when companies take that view.

One of the mainstays of the pitch made by Web3 proponents is that blockchain can democratize (or re-democratize) the web and provide new sources of wealth and opportunity—even banking the unbanked. What's your take on that?

It's a compelling pitch; I'll give them that. But crypto has so far been enormously successful at taking wealth from the average person or the financially disadvantaged and "redistributing" it to the already wealthy. The arguments I've seen for how this same technology is suddenly going to result in the democratization of wealth have been enormously uncompelling. The emerging crypto space is very poorly regulated, especially the newer parts of it pertaining to decentralized finance. It's difficult for me to see a future where poorly regulated technology with built-in perverse financial incentives will magically result in fairer, more accessible systems.

As for "banking the unbanked" and the democratization of the web, people are falling into a trap that technologists have fallen into over and over again: trying to solve social problems purely with technology. People are not unbanked because of some technological failure. People lack access to banking services for all sorts of reasons: They don't have money to open a bank account to begin with, they're undocumented, they don't have access to a physical bank or an internet or mobile connection, or they don't trust banks due to high levels of corruption in their financial or judicial systems.

These are not problems that can be solved solely through the addition of a blockchain. Indeed, crypto solutions introduce even *more* barriers: the technological know-how and the level of security practices required to safeguard a crypto wallet; the knowledge and time to try to distinguish "scammy" projects from those that are trying to be legitimate; the lack of consumer protections if something happens to an exchange where you are keeping your funds; and the added difficulty of reversing fraud when it does occur.

In my view, the places where crypto has done some good—and I do openly acknowledge that it has done some good—have primarily been in situations where there are enormous societal and political failings, and *any* replacement is better than what exists. For example, some people have successfully used crypto to send remittances to people under oppressive regimes. These examples are fairly limited, and the fact that it's worked seems largely because crypto hasn't been deployed in such a widespread way for those regimes to try to become involved.

***Given all of this, what do you think is the
cultural draw of Web3?***

The ideological argument for Web3 is very compelling, and I personally hold many of the same ideals. I *strongly* believe in working toward a more equitable and accessible financial system, creating a fairer distribution of wealth in society, supporting artists and creators, ensuring privacy and control over one's data, and democratizing access to the web. These are all things you will hear Web3 projects claiming to try to solve.

I just don't think that creating technologies based around cryptocurrencies and blockchains is the solution to these problems. These technologies build up financial barriers; they don't knock them down. They seek to introduce a layer of financialization to everything we do that I feel is, in many ways, worse than the existing systems they seek to replace. These are social and societal issues, not technological ones, and the solutions will be found in societal and political change.

Should HBR Press even be doing this book?
Are we buying into—or amplifying—the
hype cycle?

I think we are comfortably beyond the "ignore it and hope it goes away" phase of crypto. I know I decided I was beyond that phase late in 2021. I think the best thing that journalists who report on crypto can do at this stage is ask the tough questions, seek out experts wherever they can, and try not to fall for the boosterism.

Crypto and Web3 are complex on so many levels—technologically, economically, sociologically, legally—that it is difficult for any single person to report on all issues, but there are extremely competent people who have examined crypto through each of these lenses and who are asking those tough questions.

One of the biggest failures of the media in reporting on crypto has been uncritically reprinting statements from crypto boosters with little reflection on the legitimacy or feasibility of those statements. It doesn't have to be that way. That is not to say that there needs to be a double standard, either—I think most, if not all, crypto skeptics welcome pushback and critical editing of what they say and write (though I do think the financial incentive to be skeptical of crypto is dwarfed compared to the incentive to be positive about it).

Kevin Roose suggested in "The Latecomer's Guide to Crypto" in the Sunday *New York Times* in early 2022 that, in the Web 2.0 era, the early skeptics were to blame for the ills of social media because they weren't "loud enough" in their skepticism.[2] I would counter that they were not given the opportunity to be as loud as they wanted to be and that those who did hear them did not listen, or at least did not meaningfully act upon what they heard. Perhaps there is an opportunity for history not to repeat itself.

TAKEAWAYS

Web3 optimists bluster about progress on the horizon, but at present the space is rife with fraud, hacks, and collapses. Web3 critic Molly White, interviewed here by HBR, believes that as the technology becomes more mainstream, its ability to do harm—financial, emotional, and reputational—will grow, and fast.

✓ Blockchain technology is often applied in ways, or to problems, to which it is not suited, and companies frequently don't understand the consequences of their decision to utilize it.

✓ Privacy concerns around immutable records on blockchains, which could make it more difficult to address online harassment, are widely being overlooked.

✓ Despite the arguments proponents make about opportunity and democratization, crypto projects so far have mostly served the rich and powerful.

✓ Now is the moment for Web3 skeptics to raise their voices—early skeptics of the harms caused by social media in the emergence of the Web 2.0 era were not heard, and there is an opportunity not to make the same mistakes this time.

NOTES

1. Beat staff, "Kickstarter Exec on Blockchain Backlash: 'We've Learned a Hell of a Lot in the Last Couple of Months,'" Beat, February 18, 2022, https://www.comicsbeat.com/kickstarter -blockchain-controversy-interview/.

2. Kevin Roose, "The Latecomer's Guide to Crypto," *New York Times*, March 18, 2022, https://www.nytimes.com/interactive/2022 /03/18/technology/cryptocurrency-crypto-guide.html.

Adapted from content posted on hbr.org, May 10, 2022 (product #H071AM).

7

WEB3 IS OUR CHANCE TO MAKE A BETTER INTERNET

by Li Jin and Katie Parrott

O ne of the most powerful narratives surrounding
Web3 is that it is a movement toward a better, fairer
internet. Specifically, Web3 proponents envision
an internet in which users can wrest back power from a
small number of extractive, centralized institutions, and
in which everyone with an internet connection can participate on a level playing field.

But Web2, the current era of the internet defined by
companies built on proprietary data (such as Facebook

and Google), started with a similar promise of empowering individual creators and removing intermediaries—a promise left unfulfilled. Now, standing at the precipice of a new era, we should ask ourselves: Is Web3 actually democratizing opportunity? And if not, how can we better design platforms and governance systems to promote fairness?

The social and political philosopher John Rawls's thought experiment known as the "veil of ignorance," proposed in his influential 1971 work *A Theory of Justice*, provides a useful framework for these questions. When creating the foundations for an ideal society, Rawls contends, we should imagine that we do not know where we ourselves would fall within it—that is, we should adopt a veil of ignorance. A just society is one "that if you knew everything about it, you'd be willing to enter it in a random place." Rawls adds, "Among the essential features of this situation is that no one knows his place in society, his class position or social status, nor does anyone know his fortune in the distribution of natural assets and abilities, his intelligence, strength, and the like. I shall even assume that the parties do not know their conceptions of the good or their special psychological propensities."

Rawls's thought experiment is particularly relevant now because we are standing at precisely the kind of inflection point that the veil of ignorance imagines. Web3 presents the opportunity to build an entirely new internet—indeed, entire new economies—from scratch. The question then becomes: What kind of internet should we be creating?

Some might say that Web3 is young, and these issues will simply work themselves out over time. But questions about impacts and externalities were left too late in the design of Web2, with consequences ranging from election manipulation to widespread vaccine misinformation. Some indicators show that early design choices in Web3 are replicating or compounding the inequalities of Web2 and the real world.

If we want Web3 to make good on the promise that it can materially improve the situations of *everyone* within the ecosystem, and not just a handful of people at the top, we need to design it according to principles that will make that happen.

How Do We Decide What's Fair?

Philosophers and thinkers have been debating for centuries how best to allocate resources among participants in a society. The body of thought devoted to answering these questions is known as "distributive justice," and there are varying schools of thought within the discipline:

- **Strict egalitarians** argue that the only just system is one in which resources are distributed absolutely equally—in other words, everyone should have the same amount of material goods. The principle is rooted in the belief that everyone is morally equal and thus deserves to have equal access to materials and services.

- **Luck egalitarians** argue that what's important is equality of *starting* position, and that any inequalities that emerge after that point are justified by differences in merit.

- **Libertarians** argue that individual freedom should be the sole consideration, and that any effort to redistribute resources infringes on that freedom.

- **Utilitarians** argue that the most just system is the one that maximizes the sum of total happiness and well-being of all participants. Under utilitarianism, redistribution of wealth would be desirable because each additional dollar would do more to raise the well-being of a poor person than a wealthy person.

Common among these theories of justice is a tension between two equally important yet often opposing values: freedom and equality. A society in which all actors are completely free is likely to result in a significant amount of inequality, since individuals differ in their motivation to pursue wealth and will behave in ways that advance their own interests. Conversely, a society that is completely equal inhibits freedom, since individuals cannot behave in any way that causes them to be unequal to others—even if that unequal outcome is "earned" through hard work or skill.

Using veil-of-ignorance reasoning, Rawls introduced his own theory of distributive justice, known as "justice as fairness." It has two parts: the greatest equal liberty principle and the difference principle. The *greatest equal liberty principle* affords all citizens equal rights and liberties to the fullest extent that's compatible with others also having those liberties. Justice requires equal rights for every person.

The *difference principle* says that any social or economic inequalities that *do* exist in society should meet two conditions. First, they must be "attached to offices and positions open to all under conditions of fair equality and opportunity." Social positions, such as jobs, should be open to everyone and allocated by merit. In other words, a person's prospects for success should reflect their level of talent and willingness to use it, not their social class or background. And second, any inequality that does exist should maximize the benefit of the least well-off. This is a profound principle. Thus, it's acceptable that doctors earn more than janitors because that compensation differential incentivizes doctors to pursue their careers and ensures that janitors (and everyone else) will receive quality care if they fall ill.

Rawls's theory is nuanced, but in short, it's unique in how it resolves the central tension between the competing demands of freedom and equality. By requiring that inequalities benefit the least advantaged, Rawls builds in a natural corrective to the rampant inequality that would otherwise emerge in a system that privileges freedom above all else.

This balance between freedom and equality makes Rawls's theory compelling as a philosophical framework for the internet. It leaves space for builders to be rewarded for their contributions, which is necessary to foster incentives for smart, ambitious people to build in the ecosystem. At the same time, it places a burden on those builders—and the ecosystem as a whole—to build in a way that creates opportunity for less-advantaged participants.

Evaluating the Current Internet Against Justice as Fairness

How well does the current internet abide by Rawls's principles? In many ways, the Web2 internet has expanded and enhanced opportunity for a broad set of people and exists in closer accordance with Rawls's difference principle than the pre-internet world. Before the internet, access to participation in various industries was limited by a handful of gatekeepers, ranging from movie studios to music labels. The internet and social media platforms made it possible for anyone to participate in content creation and distribution, and therefore enabled more creators to succeed.

But you don't have to look far for evidence that the Web2 internet falls short of the mark in other ways. Consider just a few examples of how Web2 platforms have inhibited equality and violate the difference principle: Gig economy platforms bring in billions of dollars in revenue, while the frontline workers who deliver their services earn poverty wages and are shut out of decisions that impact their lives. Social media companies and media platforms earn billions of dollars in ad revenue from algorithmic feeds that elevate misinformation and damage vulnerable communities. Platforms' creator funds typically reward creators with the most views and engagement, leading to the concentration of income among those who already have ample sources of revenue while failing to broaden access for less-well-off aspiring creators. And we've written before about how the internet's original sin of not enabling payments led to the extractive, advertising-based business models that define the Web2 economy today.[1]

But it's not just Web2 platforms that fail to reach Rawls's standard of justice. Web3 in its current form is also exacerbating inequalities. Web3 projects commonly issue crypto tokens as digital representations of value. Early versions of token distributions have led to unsustainable dynamics wherein speculators are rewarded instead of those who are adding consistent value to networks through actual usage. Some play-to-earn games have implemented dual-token systems in which users earn income but not governance power, creating the risk of replicating the dynamics of the current economy in which workers earn salary but not equity, compounding wealth inequality. Business writer Evan Armstrong points to strong parallels between some current NFT projects and multilevel marketing schemes, in which later arrivals to the ecosystem are structurally unable to achieve the same level of success as early adopters due to system design.[2]

How to Ensure Justice as Fairness in Web3

We've seen how both the Web2 internet and early itera-tions of Web3 fall short of ensuring a free, fair playing field that benefits the least advantaged. So what would an internet that meets Rawls's standards look like? Some general anti-principles start to come into focus:

- Don't build a system that only benefits the wealthy, because what if you're poor?

- Don't build a system that disproportionately favors firstcomers, because what if you're not embedded in networks that give you early access to knowledge?

- Don't build a system that demands extreme technological savvy to succeed, because what if you don't have the aptitude or resources to learn those skills?

Using these anti-principles as guides, builders and partici-pants of the Web3 ecosystem can do three things to en-sure it aligns with Rawls's ideals of liberty, equality, and the difference principle: First, promote self-determination and agency. Second, reward participation, not just capital. And third, incorporate initiatives that benefit the disadvantaged.

Promote self-determination and agency

One of the flagship principles of Web3 is the idea of self-determination: Unlike in Web2 platforms, with a cadre of founders, executives, and shareholders holding all the power, Web3 communities will be controlled by their members. This would be consistent with economist Albert O. Hirschman's "Exit-Voice-Loyalty" model, which describes the choices individuals have when confronted with dissatisfactory situations in organizations and states. Ideally, on Web3 platforms, users can voice concerns to try to change their situation, exit to new platforms, or wait, out of loyalty, for the situation to resolve.

But the reality today is more complex. Early governance structures have largely instituted token-weighted voting, with the result being plutocracies that are not all that different from the boardrooms they're meant to be a corrective to. And the problem with plutocracy, whether it happens in a boardroom or a DAO Discord channel, is that the people holding the power are likely to look out for their own interests.

As a first step in aligning Web3's future with Rawls's principles of justice, participants and builders of the Web3 ecosystem need to push for democratic systems of governance that give a voice to all its members, not just a select few. Everyone should be equally enfranchised in the systems in which they participate.

There are additional systems of governance that can combat plutocracy, such as:

- **Reputation-based governance:** according greater governance power to those with higher reputational value

- **Delegation:** enabling community members to nominate others to vote on their behalf

- **Pods/subDAOs:** smaller groups within an organization whose scope of governance can be constrained to their missions

An example of a project purposefully diversifying its member base is Mirror's airdrop of the $WRITE token, which is needed to register a custom subdomain on the platform—and, in the future, to participate in governance. To broaden the base of users who would be able to influence governance, tokens were distributed according to an algorithm designed to maximize diverse social clusters. According to Mirror, this airdrop "further democratizes the selection process and broadens the criteria for entry. . . . [T]he expansion of the Mirror community will be determined by those who have been most integral in shaping it thus far."

Beyond the importance of voice—the ability for people to change a system from within through governance—participants also need a viable path to *exit*. Web2 platforms coerce user loyalty through network effects and closed data, and exiting a platform leaves creators without access to their audiences or content. Web3 affords the opportunity to build systems that foster user agency and self-determination through true digital ownership, open data, and networks that are built atop open-source software.

Reward participation, not just capital

A core philosophical tenet of Web3 is that there are more ways to provide value to an ecosystem than through capital, and furthermore, that value should be able to be earned, not just purchased. This is a radical departure from the existing structure, where those with capital earn more through investments than people can earn through work, resulting in a widening wealth gap over time.

Distribution of ownership to participants is also a major shift away from how incumbent platforms are built, wherein meaningful ownership accrues to employees and investors but excludes users whose content and contributions make those platforms valuable.

An important step in aligning Web3 with the principles of justice as fairness is to ensure that everyone is on
an equal footing and can attain positions of power or
compensation through their own merit and contributions. The reality so far has been that those in the right
knowledge networks can compound their wealth through
strategies like creating multiple accounts (known as "sybil
farming") to receive additional token airdrops. And while
early distributions of tokens often perversely incentivized
short-term mercenary behavior—like participating in
yield farms and then exiting them days later in search of
higher yields—there is an opportunity to iterate and improve the process to support networks' long-term retention
and sustainability. One way is by making it possible to earn
ownership through ongoing participation in networks,
not just capital investment. Projects that are working to
expand access to ownership include RabbitHole, Layer3,
Gitcoin, BanklessDAO, and FWB.

Incorporate initiatives that benefit
the disadvantaged

The difference principle is grounded in the idea that
inequality, per se, is not a bad thing. With fair equality
of opportunity as a prerequisite, inequality remains an

inevitable outcome of people's natural abilities and level of desire and effort to earn money. But when inequalities do arise, do those arrangements benefit those less privileged in society?

This is a challenging principle to apply in the context of technology. But consider this thought exercise: Do the current social networking feed algorithms promote content that maximizes the benefit to the least well-off? For platform creator funds that give payments to content creators, predicated on views and engagement: Do such inequalities in payouts maximize the benefit to the least well-off among their users? The answer is likely no. While top creators have a plethora of ways to monetize and can sustain their output regardless of creator fund payouts, the least well-off may not even participate in content creation due to financial constraints.

The difference principle will be particularly important to the democratization of Web3, since participants will enter the ecosystem at different times with a wide variety of backgrounds, incomes, and technological fluency and access. There are already many examples of projects leveraging crypto to maximize the well-being of the least well-off. For example, SuperHi, a for-profit creative education platform that is planning to decentralize ownership to its members and instructors, tested a basic income program with the goal of broadening access to creative careers. Projects like Proof of Humanity and ImpactMarket seek to use blockchain technology as a foundation to provide basic income to those in need. Communities like LaborDAO are leveraging building blocks to build worker power, while others like she256, We3, and Komorebi Collective are focused on increasing diversity in the blockchain space.

Besides projects that have social good as an explicit mission, all Web3 networks should be incentivized to adhere to the difference principle and maximize benefit to the least well-off, since that approach maximizes attractiveness to new participants, propelling further network effects.

A Fair, Just Internet Is Possible

Web3 offers the opportunity for a meaningful course correction—a chance to reimagine the internet and build new platforms from first principles. But in order to do that, we need to agree on what those principles should be, and why. Rawls's principles of justice provide a useful starting point. Without full knowledge of where our positions will be, our aim should be to design new systems rooted in fairness and consideration for all.

TAKEAWAYS

Web3 presents a chance to reimagine the internet with fresh principles. The *difference principle*, proposed by the political philosopher John Rawls, says that any social or economic inequalities that exist in society should be attached to an individual's talent and societal impact. Builders and participants of Web3 can do three things to ensure it aligns with these ideals.

✓ Promote self-determination and agency. Builders and participants should push for democratic systems of governance that give a voice and equal enfranchisement to all members.

✓ Reward participation, not just capital. They should ensure that everyone is on an equal footing and can attain positions of power or compensation through their own merit and contributions.

✓ Incorporate initiatives that benefit the disadvantaged. All Web3 networks should be incentivized to maximize benefit to the least well-off. This

approach increases attractiveness to new participants, propelling further network effects.

NOTES

1. Li Jin and Katie Parrott, "The Web3 Renaissance: A Golden Age for Content," *Li's Newsletter* (blog), December 20, 2021, https:// every.to/means-of-creation/the-web3-renaissance-a-golden-age -for-content.

2. Evan Armstrong, "NFT Projects Are Just MLMs for Tech Elites," *Napkin Math* (blog), September 30, 2021, https://every.to /napkin-math/nft-projects-are-just-mlms-for-tech-elites.

Adapted from content posted on hbr.org, May 10, 2022 (product #H070U9).

About the Contributors

ANA ANDJELIC is a strategy executive and the author of *The Business of Aspiration*. She also runs a newsletter, *The Sociology of Business*.

REID BLACKMAN is the author of *Ethical Machines: Your Concise Guide to Totally Unbiased, Transparent, and Respectful AI* (Harvard Business Review Press, 2022) and founder and CEO of Virtue, an ethical-risk consultancy. He is also a senior adviser to the Deloitte AI Institute, previously served on Ernst & Young's AI Advisory Board, and volunteers as the chief ethics officer to the nonprofit Government Blockchain Association. Previously, Reid was a professor of philosophy at Colgate University and the University of North Carolina, Chapel Hill.

JAD ESBER is the cofounder of koodos, a New York–based Web3 company, and is affiliated with Harvard's Berkman Klein Center for Internet & Society and The New School's Institute for the Cooperative Digital Economy. He builds, writes, and speaks on the topic of social spaces and creative tools and the intersections with decentralized technologies. Previously, he worked at Google and YouTube, where he worked with and built for creators and artists in emerging markets. Follow him on Twitter @jad_ae.

RAMSEY KHABBAZ is an associate editor at *Harvard Business Review*.

SCOTT DUKE KOMINERS is the MBA Class of 1960 Associate Professor of Business Administration in the Entrepreneurial Management Unit at Harvard Business School, and a faculty affiliate of the Harvard Department of Economics. He is also an a16z crypto research partner and advises a number of companies on marketplace and incentive design. Previously, he was a junior fellow at the Harvard Society of Fellows and the inaugural Saieh Family Fellow in Economics at the Becker Friedman Institute. Follow him on Twitter @skominers.

LI JIN is a cofounder and general partner of Variant, a venture capital firm focused on investing in Web3 and the ownership economy. She writes a newsletter about the future of work and consumer technology at li.substack.com.

ANDREW MCAFEE is the cofounder of the Initiative on the Digital Economy at the MIT Sloan School of Management. He is a coauthor of *The Second Machine Age* and *Machine, Platform, Crowd.*

KATIE PARROTT is a writer and editor at Every, a media company publishing essays and analysis focusing on business.

JEFF JOHN ROBERTS is crypto editor at *Fortune* and the author of *Kings of Crypto: One Startup's Quest to Take Cryptocurrency out of Silicon Valley and onto Wall Street* (Harvard Business Review Press, 2020). His work has appeared in a variety of other outlets, including *Bloomberg BusinessWeek*, Reuters, and the *New York Times.* He is an authority on copyright law and other intellectual property issues and is licensed to practice law in New York and Ontario. He has appeared on the BBC, CNN, NBC, CheddarTV, and other outlets to share his perspectives on technology and the law. Follow him on Twitter @jeffjohnroberts.

JONATHAN RUANE is a lecturer in the global economics and management group at the MIT Sloan School of Management and a research scientist at MIT's Initiative on the Digital Economy.

THOMAS STACKPOLE is a senior editor at *Harvard Business Review*.

MOLLY WHITE is a software developer, Wikipedia editor, and the creator of the website Web3 Is Going Just Great.

Index

Is Your Business Ready for the Future?

If you enjoyed this book and want more on today's pressing business topics, turn to other books in the **Insights You Need** series from *Harvard Business Review*. Featuring HBR's latest thinking on topics critical to your company's success—from Blockchain and Cybersecurity to AI and Agile—each book will help you explore these trends and how they will impact you and your business in the future.